I0445393

EXERCISE YOUR
M.I.G.H.T.

HOW TO LIVE THE ABUNDANT LIFE GOD PROMISED YOU!

PASTOR RICK STEPHENSON

WISDOM WELL

Exercise Your M.I.G.H.T.: How to Live the Abundant Life God Promised You!

Copyright © 2022–Rick Stephenson

WISDOM WELL

Unless otherwise indicated, all scriptural quotations are taken from The Holy Bible, King James Version, Copyright © 1994 by Zondervan Publishing House, Grand Rapids, MI. All rights reserved.

Scripture quotations marked NIV are taken from the Holy Bible, New International Version®, NIV®. Copyright © 1984 by Biblica, Inc.™ Used by permission of Zondervan.

Paperback ISBN: 979-8-9858122-0-6
eBook ISBN: 979-8-9858122-1-3

Cover Design: 99Designs.com
Page Design and Layout: Jodi Giddings
Editor: Tina Pocernich—Wandering Words Media

Library of Congress Control Number: 2022904501

All rights reserved. No part of this publication may be reproduced, distributed, or transmitted in any form or by any means, electronic or mechanical, including photocopying and recording, or by any information storage and retrieval system without the prior written permission of the publisher, except in the case of brief quotations embodied in critical reviews and certain other noncommercial uses permitted by copyright law.

Although the author and publisher have made every effort to ensure that the information in this publication was correct at press time, the author and publisher do not assume and hereby disclaim any liability to any party for any loss, damage, or disruption caused by errors or omissions, whether such errors or omissions result from negligence, accident, or any other cause. Any perceived slight of any individual or organization is purely unintentional.

The resources in this publication are provided for informational purposes only and should not be used to replace the specialized training and professional judgment of a health care or mental health care professional.

Neither the author nor the publisher can be held responsible for the use of the information provided within this publication. Please always consult a trained professional before making any decision regarding treatment of yourself or others.

For more information, email **Rick-Stephenson@wisdomwell.guru.**

A FREE GIFT FOR YOU

SUBSCRIBE TO THE NEWSLETTER AND RECEIVE A FREE BOOKLET!

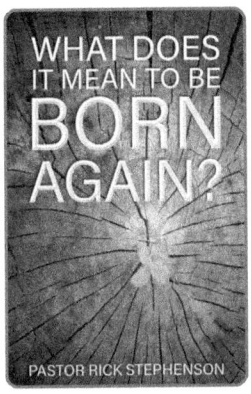

Have you ever wondered what Jesus meant when he said, "You must be born again," found in the Gospel of John chapter three?

You've likely heard many interpretations of this scripture, and it's a good idea to make sure for yourself that you have indeed been born again according to the manner in which God intended.

Remove all doubt by reading this brief, contemporary and easy-to-comprehend booklet, written by Pastor Rick Stephenson. In this conversational and relatable booklet, Pastor Rick walks you through the true Biblical meaning behind what it means to be born again.

YOU WILL LEARN:

- How Jesus's words of spiritual birth are related to physical birth.
- The extensive process God uses for bringing about new birth in a believer.
- The exclusive proof that validates the new birth experience has happened to you.
- What is expected of a believer once they have been born again.

Understanding the words of Jesus will move you into a deeper, more meaningful relationship with God and allow you to experience the new birth in a full, enriching, and rewarding manner.

Begin the journey to discover what it means to be born again by reading this amazing booklet now!

Sign up today by visiting **www.WisdomWell.guru/newsletter**

DEDICATION

To my wife Julie, who has filled my life with abundance. You have been an amazing partner on this journey of life. I simply cannot imagine having made it this far without you. You have been a shining example of what it means to live from a place of abundance because your heart is constantly overflowing with generosity and love.

To Abigail, who truly is your father's joy. You are an incredibly wonderful daughter who takes after your mother with an outpouring of kindness. You have added richness to my life simply because I can say I am your dad. I am so excited to see how God uses your life to share the abundance he allows to flow through you to others since you have a knack for giving of yourself away with such charity.

To Aaron, you amaze me with your abundance of discipline and confidence. God has truly made you to overflow with ability and passion. I am learning so much from your drive and determination to improve and help others. I am truly blessed to not only call you son but also friend.

To Jesus, my God and my Savior, thank you for teaching me your point of view on abundance, so I could benefit from God's economy of giving rather than receiving. You have saved me, grown me, and now it's time to pour me out to help with the harvest of abundance.

CONTENTS

INTRODUCTION

I'VE GOT TO FIND *something to use. Something sturdy*, my nine-year-old self thought as I searched around my room frantically. *Something that won't break and that I can tighten... There's got to be something here, something that will work.*

Then it caught my eye: a thick, shiny, black leather belt.

How fitting. That's it. I'll use that!

I knew the familiar black belt all too well. Not necessarily *this* belt, since this one was mine, but the belt of my former foster father.

After being placed in a foster home at the age of three, I lived with my foster parents, three boys—two who were several years older than me and one a little younger than me—as well as a girl, who may have been about my own age. I assume those children were theirs since I stood out like a sore thumb compared to the rest of them in pictures. They were all fair-skinned and blonde headed, while I was darker in complexion with a dark brown head of hair. I don't remember all the details because I was young and shut down after my experiences there.

How did I get to know that infamous black belt, you may ask? I don't know if it was the stress of a large family or the alcohol that drove him to it, but that belt found its way across my back more times than I can count. My foster father may have been aiming for my butt, but because of my tiny stature at three years old (or because of the alcohol I mentioned previously), it often missed its mark and landed somewhere along my back.

Now, don't feel too sorry for me—I wasn't the only one singled out with this particular discipline for something I may have done wrong (or more likely, for something *contrived* that I did wrong). Really, you should feel sorry for all five of us kids, because if any one of us did something wrong, we were all lined up and endured punishment together. He claimed since no one would own up to the crime, we all would suffer the same sentence. However, even if someone did admit to having trespassed in some way, it really didn't matter. It still became a so-called "learning opportunity" for the rest of us.

Sometimes to make the occasion more intense, besides the over-abundance of yelling that went along with these episodes, he cracked the belt beforehand. He doubled up the belt so that there were two layers, one on top of the other, then pushed it together to expand it before pulling his hands away quickly so it flew back in place, creating a sharp cracking sound.

Other times, the punishment wasn't so well planned and organized, rather it was more a case of his jumping off the couch, clutching at his waist to grab the belt, then using it as a whip to carry out immediate justice.

Yes, I endured this and other similar "pleasantries" in this foster home for almost four years, but that wasn't the only thing that had me now searching my messy bedroom for my own black leather belt. It was only *one* part. I was impacted further by life with my adoptive family, which was the other part of what drove my search.

After my survival at the hands of my foster caretakers, I was miraculously adopted at the age of seven. Back in the early 1970s, it was rare for couples to want to adopt a toddler, let alone a school age child. Mostly, they wanted babies and if they could not get a baby, they would settle for a child under the age of five. So, it really was unique for a couple to come and talk to me at almost seven years old about making me a part of their family (just the three of us).

As I mentioned, my recollection of events is very sparse. I truly only recall a few events from the foster home and a few more from the time I'll call my "transition" from foster home to adopted home. But I do know I felt very strange about the whole thing and thought everything seemed to be happening very fast—way too fast for an almost seven-year-old to understand.

The one thing I know for sure is on the day of the adoption, we were in a courtroom, and I was asked by the lawyer if I wanted to be adopted by this couple.

My only questions to him were, "What happens if I say no? Do I have to go back to the foster home?"

Wow. Pause a minute and think about that. That was pretty smart for a seven-year-old, if I do say so myself. Looking back, I am a little sad that an overwhelming, "yes," didn't come out of my mouth. If I had the understanding then as I do now, at almost fifty-five years of age, I would have seen the warning buried within my response. There must have been something I sensed that caused me to hesitate and understand that even this new situation wasn't going to be ideal. I only wanted to know, by means of my inquiry, whether my life was at least going to improve over my current situation. I think this is the main question we all have when we face major life changes, like deciding who to marry, choosing whether to have children, or change jobs. We want to know if our life is going to be better as a result of the decision we have to make.

The answer I got was that if I said no to the adoption, I would be placed back into a foster home—but not necessarily the same one. Well, that did it for me, because it simply became a choice between three options: one which I clearly knew, one that I had a pretty good idea about after having spent a few weeks or months getting familiar with this new couple (I really don't know how much time the process took. I just know we got together a few times and I saw their house.), and lastly a new option of which I knew nothing. At the time, facing the unknown was scarier than going back to the same foster home, and the same foster home was worse than moving on to something with which I was somewhat familiar, so the only response I could settle upon was a simple, "OK," for the adoption.

Over approximately the next three years, what transpired may have been just as bad as what I experienced in the previous four. I was no longer physically abused, but now I encountered a constant barrage of emotional beatings. I can't recall all the words my adopted mother addressed to me, but the general gist was that I was stupid, worthless, and would never amount to anything.

Again, I can't put my finger on what may have caused it. Perhaps it was the daily stress of my adopted mother's job as a learning disabilities teacher that exhausted her. Alternatively, it could have been the difficulty of raising someone else's kid—because I was no angel. Regardless of the cause, since my adoptive father was a phlegmatic pacifist who hid in his office in the basement, I was left without an advocate to defend me during these verbal whippings. So, after a few years of this emotional abuse, I was empty, lonely, and defeated.

So, here I was at nine years old thinking, *If this is love, then I don't want anything to do with it! If this is all there is to this life, either physical or emotional abuse, then I'm done with it! If no one wants me anyway, then what am I doing here?* which had me searching my room for something to hang myself. I went to my room, closed the door, and searched, finally deciding the belt would do the job. I sat down on the edge of the bed, wrapped the belt around my neck, and slid it through the buckle tight enough that it was now choking me.

Next, I thought, *I've got to wrap the other end around something.*

Through the tears beginning to flood my eyes, I saw the closet hanging rod and thought I would try that, but it didn't seem high enough for me to hang.

While I was thinking this through, suddenly I heard a voice—not an external, audible voice, but a voice deep within me. I did not recognize the voice, but I knew for certain it wasn't mine. I had never heard this voice before, but it had authority and warmth in it. There was compassion in its tone.

All it said was, "Don't do it."

Those words struck me and caused me to undo the belt from around my neck. It was a pivotal moment in my life which gave me what I can only identify as hope. It was then I started my journey toward God. I did not know that at the time, of course, since I was too young to truly comprehend it or to even think about it in those terms. All I knew was the voice had just saved my life.

Since then, I've learned a lot on this journey of life. I've learned how to overcome battles with depression, change my self-talk and thought life, build meaningful relationships, take care of my physical health, and even master my finances. I've also repaired my relationship with my adoptive parents so that today it's healthier and satisfying. Most importantly, I've learned how to communicate with and center my life around God. In fact, I even became a licensed minister.

After years in ministry and seeing how God has worked through me to uplift others with what I've learned, I felt strongly led to write this book with the intention of helping as many people as possible experience what God can do for them.

Allow me to share a little more about my background and why I believe I can speak to the things included in this book. Over the past thirty-two years, I graduated from the University of Wisconsin-Eau Claire with an accounting degree, and subsequently obtained my professional qualifications as a Certified Public Accountant and Certified Management Accountant. I worked as an internal auditor for an international service company for a while, then as a public auditor at one of the top nationwide accounting firms. Next, I obtained my real estate license and became a general manager and controller for a large real estate development company. With my business experience,

I became a business consultant and gained further experience over the years in several industries, including insurance, utilities, manufacturing, state government, financial services, and others. I also obtained certification as a master financial coach. I think it is reasonable to say I understand financial matters and business, but how did this lead to a spiritual-based book?

Growing up in my adopted home, I attended church services with my parents every weekend. Additionally, every weekday morning while I was in high school, we went to mass. Ever since my encounter with the "voice," I was drawn to spiritual things. I would pick up my Bible (which had been given to me by someone as an adoption gift) and read it on my own, without anyone prompting me to do so. The stories I read stuck with me. In fact, everyone who knew me as I was growing up assumed I would become a Catholic priest. However, my experiences growing up fostered a desire to have my own family whom I could love and who would love me, so being a priest was out of the question.

Nonetheless, God kept tugging at my heart from childhood through college, and this eventually led me to a Bible study, where he revealed himself to me through his word. After the first lesson, it was as if a search light was turned on in my mind and heart. Things finally began making sense as to why I experienced what I did. As a result of that Bible study, I committed myself to God and shortly thereafter, he prompted me to obtain licensure as a minister. For the past twenty years, I have been involved in ministry. I have led Bible studies, done street preaching, held roles as a church music director, and been a worship leader. I have spent years doing prison ministry and holding evangelistic services. I am also an avid musician and songwriter. I have released contemporary Christian music albums of my own original songs, several of which have found their way to radio stations in my home of the US as well as overseas.

I believe God allowed me to experience a very unique background so I might understand the things I will be sharing in this book.

In John 10:10, Jesus said, **"The thief cometh not, but for to steal, and to kill, and to destroy: I am come that they might have life, and that they might have it more abundantly."** This scripture is the basis of the book you are about to read.

Unfortunately, this scripture has not been adequately understood nor explained in a way for most to properly comprehend it. Therefore, its promises are seldom discovered. I believe God has helped me to not only grasp it, but to also live it—and now share it with you.

I can honestly say I have lived and will continue to live an abundant life! You might wonder at that statement, after just reading a little about my past, but I want to assure you I truly mean it. That is because I have come to understand what abundance in every area of our lives looks like from *God's* viewpoint, not my own.

I know some people encourage others to "live your best life now," or to seek the prosperity of God for every area of your life. They paint a rosy picture of having success in life by living for God and asking him for what you want. However, the kind of image they paint is only one that makes you feel good but doesn't help you make sense of the challenges, difficulties, or pain and trauma you may have already experienced (or are yet to experience). After all, how does *that* fit into an abundant life?

The truth is, you can't have one without the other.

It is my desire to help you understand not only why an abundant life is important and what it takes to acquire it, but how to maintain it. I want to help you understand how all your experiences work together to shape a life of abundance, so I wrote this book to help you understand what an "abundant life" means to God. It's sort of a what-I-wish-I-knew-then book, written in hopes that you won't struggle like I did.

I believe everyone has a purpose to fulfill, and if we miss the fulfillment of our purpose, the world is missing out on us. Additionally, I believe it is a part of everyone's purpose to experience the abundance Jesus said we could have, because it's through abundance that we can impact others for good. Most people will never consider their purpose and how it plays out in their lives. However, since you're reading this book and you've come this far already, you must be looking to fulfill your special purpose. Therefore, it is my intent to help you understand how experiencing abundance can help you in your fulfillment.

Together, we will consider what true abundance from God's point of view means. We will also discuss how to maintain that abundance. So, please continue reading, and discover for yourself how God's abundance can help shape your life.

1
DEFINING THE PROBLEM

"The end of life is not to be happy, nor to achieve pleasure and avoid pain, but to do the will of God, come what may."
—Rev. Martin Luther King Jr.

SHE YELLED AT ME, "You will never amount to much." I don't know why she screamed that time, but my adoptive mother followed up with that phrase after previously calling me stupid. I am sure as a pre-teen, teenager, or even as a young adult I did a lot of stupid things. In fact, I have done and continue to do a lot of stupid things, but I knew in my heart that I wasn't stupid. I remember one time yelling back at her, "I am not stupid," which rewarded me with a slap in the face.

It wasn't the slap across my face or even being called stupid which hurt the most. Rather, it was those lingering words, "You will never amount to much," that stung and left a mark. Many times I thought to myself, "I'll show her!" But why— why did I have that response? Why did I want to "show" her? Why did I want to succeed and prove her wrong? Was it only out of spite—to prove myself worthy—just to show I could?

I believe there is something within all of us that wants to be successful at this thing called life. We all want others to look at us and understand we did it, we accomplished everything we set out to do, and we were good at something. There's a drive within us to count or matter in some way. Perhaps it's because we want to leave more than a simple inheritance. We want to leave a mark, a legacy, an impact when we're gone, or some history demonstrating we made a difference because we were here and because of the life we lived.

However, to feel that we lived effectively, we need an understanding of the word life. Is life simply the act of breathing in and out all day long from the day we are born into this world until we take our last breath and exit it? I think I hear a unanimous, "No!" from everyone.

Life is something more, but how do we define it? Ask a thousand people what life means to them, and you'll likely receive a thousand slightly, if not altogether different, answers. Looking for answers in the dictionary does not provide much help either since it says *life* is "the condition that distinguishes animals and plants from inorganic matter, including the capacity for growth, reproduction, functional activity, and continual change preceding death."[1] Yes, life is certainly at least that! (Notice that the dictionary didn't even specify a separate classification of humans in its definition, so it must lump us in with animals. While I love my pets and appreciate animals for their uniqueness, that still doesn't sit well with me, and it shouldn't with you either—we are so much more than that!)

Perhaps we can still glean something from the definition that life is made up of "continual change." I think we all know the one thing we can count on, the one thing that never varies in this life is…change. If life is made up of constant change, then hopefully it is primarily made up of changes meant to improve us. (While not every change seems good at first, if we pause a moment and examine our response, maybe we can see some good within every change, if not immediately then

DEFINING THE PROBLEM

at least over time—read Romans 8:28.) Could we say life is a path of continuous growth—a journey of discovery? If so, growth in what areas of our lives?

Our lives involve many facets of our makeup like our friendships, work, feelings, thoughts, significant others, money, and so on. So, where do we focus, or do we realize it's an intertwining ball of string that is impossible to unravel and therefore work on it all at once?

We must continue to grow and change for the better in every area of our lives. My personal slogan to help motivate myself to pursue continual growth since college is "moving and improving." When something is not moving forward, it is standing still, or it's sliding backward and losing ground, or decaying. Even when we think that things are as good as they can get, there is always a way to enhance or improve life. Some will hold on to the adage, "If it ain't broke, don't fix it." However, there are others that say, "If it ain't broke, then break it to find an even better way." It's those people who have found tremendous success in various avenues of life.

I also believe this is the attitude God is looking for in people. He wants to know we want more out of this life (and in our relationship with him), and when things get complacent that we will shake it up and say, "How can we enhance it and improve?" You see we were designed by our Creator to be successful. Jeremiah 29:11 tells us, **"For I know the plans I have for you, declares the Lord, plans to prosper you and not to harm you, plans to give you hope and a future."** (NIV)

Based on this scripture's use of the word "prosper," we can conclude God desires abundance for us. The actual Hebrew word used is *šālôm* (pronounced shaw-lome') and we know it better translated as "peace." However, it also means "welfare, health, safety or soundness, friendship or relationship, and of course prosperity."[2] This complete definition implies God has every area of our lives in his best interest. Yes, I said *his* best interest rather than ours, since God is looking out for each of us—meaning he's concerned with how we fit into *all* of his creation. When we think of our best interest, it typically involves only ourselves to the exclusion of others. According to this scripture and this word, we know God wants us to experience abundance and prosper in life. But to have abundance, we must understand what abundance truly means or how would we know when we've obtained it?

Most of us pursue prosperity, whether we know God or not, because the desire is built within. It's a feature of our design. We pursue all life has to offer. We start out with our best foot forward, striving to be successful at something on which we've set our heart, but then, as they say, "life happens." Something gets in the way, we get knocked down, off course, and unfocused. We find ourselves floundering in the ocean of self-doubt and struggle to find the life raft of hope. When others have said things to us like, "you'll never amount to much," even if we grab hold of a lifeline, our grip is weak. The weight of these negative statements is tied to our psyche and we struggle with accomplishment.

SO WHY?

Why write another book about living an abundant life? This actually is my first book about the topic, but from a reader's perspective, why read another one when there are so many available? I believe I have a unique insight to share with you, which I learned from spending decades falling, getting back up, and trying over and over, all the while developing my relationship with God so he could guide me, teach me, correct me, and help me finally "get it."

Saying I "get it" can be a bit of a stretch, but I truly believe that I finally understand a few things about myself that has made my journey a bit more relatable and enjoyable. Do I know everything about everything? Of course not—far from it! But what I do know, I wish I had known many years ago so I would have avoided some pitfalls and heartache along the way. Maybe I wouldn't have taken those words spoken over me so personally. That's what I'm hoping, at a minimum, this book will do for you. I hope it inspires you to build a deeper more meaningful relationship with God, as you pursue the abundant life along with the plans and purpose he has for you.

I'm not saying you don't have a very good relationship with God already—I really hope you do. But by sharing our thoughts and ideas, we can motivate each other to think about things in ways we may not have otherwise, and in turn bring about exponential growth and development within ourselves.

The apostle Paul wrote in his first epistle to the Corinthians, **"For now we see through a glass, darkly; but then face to face: now I know in part; but then shall I know even as also I am known."** (1 Corinthians 13:12)

I think he was emphasizing that no one knows everything here on this earth, because we do not have complete access to heavenly perfection. Instead, we are all learning and growing as we stumble along life's journey. Therefore, let's understand we are all working on this thing called life together, but also notice something else in Paul's phrase. It's a key that if we can turn it, will unlock something for us. Paul says that we are already known by God. (Well, obviously, you say!) Yes, God knows us because he designed us—but that's not the key. The *key* is just before he says, "then shall I know." What shall we know? Ourselves!

We shall know ourselves just like God already knows us. How do we know this is true? Because the word "glass" used in this scripture is actually a Greek word *esoptron* (pronounced es'-op-tron) which can be also translated as a "mirror."[3] Who do you see in a mirror when you look? Yourself! The first step toward an abundant life comes from knowing yourself.

However, it can be difficult to truly know ourselves. Jeremiah 17:9 points out, **"The heart is deceitful above all things, and desperately wicked: who can know it?"** In really knowing ourselves, we must be brutally honest with ourselves.

LET'S BE HONEST

If you are anything like me, and you probably are, you may have found that at various times you were so focused on a certain area of your life you felt like you were killing it, so to speak. I remember a few years into my career, I felt like I was finally connecting the dots between my college education and my work and it finally made sense. I was working hard and making good money. I bought a few snazzy suits and looked good too, so I thought I was successful—and at that moment, perhaps I was.

But then something happened. I got into a relationship and suddenly things shifted. I was more concerned with building this new relationship than my work. I knew I needed to continue to do a good job at work, but as I dove into the new possibilities with my relationship interest, I was starting to struggle.

As the relationship deepened, things from my past that I thought were tucked away or buried rose to new life and demanded to be dealt with once again. When I tried navigating this rising turmoil, my work really began to suffer.

I realized I wasn't as successful as I once thought. Like a circus performer spinning all sorts of plates at one time then adding a new plate to the mix, I was off beat, and likely to drop all my plates. I began thinking, *how do others handle it all?*

After we married, it magnified certain things and then as I became a parent, I really felt inadequate. Again, thoughts of, *how do people cope and expect to be good at all of this?* flooded my being.

There seems to be this expectation in the world that you should be successful at whatever is going on in your life (that is, your work, your relationships, your health, your money, etc.), but so few are successful in every part of their lives. Sure, many get focused on an area or two and find a certain amount of success. They may dedicate themselves to work and put in extraordinary hours and find some reward in financial terms, but at home their marriages are falling apart, their kids won't talk to them, or their health is failing because they're not taking care of their bodies.

I wanted to know how to manage it all. In my pursuit of the answer, I found all sorts of recommendations to help me improve and be successful in life, but I also found they missed the mark. Many times, I asked myself, "How can I be a good husband and father, bring home the bacon, stay in shape, build for my future, and do all the other things I know I need to do?" I tried to pivot and focus on a certain area of my life, then when something else in my life was suffering from lack of attention, I pivoted to that, perhaps spending time with my kids and when that improved, then I tried to eat better, but each time I got focused on one area, another suffered.

Many told me it was all about time management. I tried all the tricks I picked up from books or seminars for better management of my schedule and I made some small gains, but as demands increased I ended up right back in the same place. Others said it was about discipline and determination, so I wrote affirmations to myself, tried to implement routines, and committed to myself that no matter what, I wouldn't give up—but once more life threw new pressures and challenges at me that caused failures and disappointments.

Still others said it was all about balance. So, I tried using everything I learned up to that point, but I discovered when something was out of balance, you had to decide what you were going to release to get back into balance.

Balance in life can be equated to a teeter-totter. When I was growing up almost every playground had them. Today's playgrounds have all sorts of fancy jungle gyms instead, so most kids today don't know how much fun they were. You would get on one end of the teeter-totter while your friend got on the other end. If you were both approximately the same size or weight, the teeter-totter bounced back and forth so each of you got a turn being up in the air and then rushing back down to feel your tummy jump.

It was a lot of fun until you were doing it with someone who was much bigger than you. They could mercilessly hold you up in the air if they wanted to and there wasn't much you could do about it. Often your only option was to jump off and risk getting hurt. Sometimes you could find a four-person teeter-totter with two planks positioned in the shape of a plus sign where four people could sit and wobble up and down and even a little side to side based on the center weight. However, if you only had two other friends, one of the three of you would have the advantage of controlling the other two.

THE LESSON

This is what it's like trying to find balance in life. Life should not be a balancing act, because to find the right amount of balance, you must determine how much weight are you going to put on each end. In other words, on what are you going to place your importance? If you place a certain emphasis on one end but not the same emphasis on the other end, then one side is going to be higher or more successful than the other.

To fix the problem, you could adjust the weight or move the fulcrum, that is the spot or point at which the pivot or support of the weight occurs. This solution only works for a little while because it places too much stress at the point of the fulcrum if it's not aligned in the center. Consider life as more like the four-person teeter-totter than the two-person because there are several areas we must balance. However, even on the four-person version, moving the fulcrum is not really an option. Therefore, the only real solution is adjusting the weight.

This got me thinking that if the only way to manage all the things in life is to find the proper balance with the proper weight on all aspects being the same, then how can you possibly achieve success in every area of life? Don't we want the most life has to offer, and if so, then does that mean something always has to be out of balance? It also got me thinking, is that what God asks of us? To be out of balance? I don't think so. I think he wants the opposite for us—to be in balance *and* to have all we want out of life. I found a particular scripture tumbling around in my head and I really wanted to know its meaning.

The thief cometh not, but for to steal, and to kill, and to destroy: I am come that they might have life, and that they might have it more abundantly. (John 10:10)

If Jesus offers us abundant life and I have accepted Jesus into my life, then why isn't my life abundant? That's when the next realization hit me. It's in letting go that you begin to determine what abundance means to you. Adjusting the weight in the teeter-totter of life means that you must shift your priorities—what matters most to you. This is part of the process of getting to know yourself. Abundance isn't about having everything—that's called greed and greed is a selfish motive.

Abundance is about coming to terms with yourself and realizing that you are not entitled to everything, that you can have enough and then some—and you certainly don't need to hoard it all. When you understand that simple concept, letting go of some things becomes easier.

For example, for a long time I thought I wanted a boat. My wife grew up on lakes, boating with her family, and I thought that would be fun and exciting. I strove to make enough money to afford one, but I could never accumulate enough because there were always other demands upon my money. When I finally realized I am not a boat person, because I wouldn't want the headache of maintaining it, storing it, and cleaning it, I let go of that desire and the stress that came along with striving for it. This is a very simple example, but it truly works in every area of our lives.

When we determine to know, really know, who we are, who God designed us to be, then we can start to assess what is important in our lives. When we understand what is important to us, then we can begin to let go of what is not important and gain a sense of balance.

As we move forward in this book, we are going to learn what abundance means in every area of our lives from God's point of view. And we're going to see that abundance not only benefits us as individuals and our relationship with God, but it benefits others. We're also going to understand what we are to do with abundance once we have it and how we maintain it as we keep "moving and improving."

As a side note, we must also realize life does not end when we take our last breath here on earth. I believe it continues in what some would call the great beyond, the afterlife, or heaven. I have read not only the Bible, but hundreds, if not thousands of near-death experiences (stories of those who died and were brought back to this physical life), and it has shown me that there is more than meets the eye to this thing we call life.

TAKE AWAYS

- Words make a difference (those we speak to others and those we speak to ourselves)—they can motivate or deflate. It depends on how you interpret them.

- We all want to live an impactful life and make a difference for having been here upon this earth, even if it's for just one other person (our spouse, children, relatives, or friends).

- Life is made up of continual change meant to make us better. We are meant to keep "moving and improving."

- God has plans to prosper us or allow us to experience abundance in every area of our lives, and we must know what that means from God's perspective, not our own.

- We all face challenges and struggles and we need each other to help us make it through them—but most importantly, we need a good relationship with God to help make sense of them.

- The first step toward an abundant life comes from knowing yourself, and that can be difficult. Therefore, it requires brutal honesty.

- There are numerous recommendations and techniques available to help us improve and be successful in this life, but it takes more than following recommendations and techniques. It requires us to have balance, which means determining upon what are you going to place importance, and in that determination, you also must decide of what to let go. Then you begin to understand what abundance means to you.

- Jesus promises us an abundant life. However, abundance isn't about having everything—that's called greed and greed is a selfish motive. Abundance is about coming to terms with yourself.

NEXT STEPS

I encourage you to look at what areas in your life feel out of balance. What have you been striving for or struggling with that you need to let go of to find a sense of balance? It's in that place of balance where true abundance will begin to become clearer to you. You will begin to shift from the place of selfishness to a place of genuine centeredness. Eventually we need to be focused on others, but that is impossible and unhealthy until we have authentically centered ourselves first. We are, after all, our own fulcrum. To pivot this life correctly we first must get to know ourselves so spend some time deeply thinking about who you are as a person.

TRANSITION

Now that we understand abundance must start with balance and balance must start with understanding ourselves—who we are, what we are, what we desire—we can discover what abundance truly means. We can define abundance, not in our terms, but rather in God's terms for us. So, let's proceed with the next chapter and begin defining abundance.

2
ABUNDANCE DEFINED

"Riches are not from abundance of worldly goods,
but from a contented mind."

–Unknown

Take a deep breath in and out. Slowly. Go ahead... Really...
I'll wait.

Take in one more deep breath—and release it. Do it very slowly
and very purposefully.

What did you feel? Perhaps you noticed how your chest
expanded during the slow purposeful inhalation of air. Maybe
you felt your heart rate slow for a moment. Or you may have
felt the release of a tiny bit of stress as you exhaled. In any case,
you should have felt something—otherwise, you might be
dead. I asked you to take that deep breath to prove one thing.
You are alive, and if you are alive, then this book is for you.

Most of us have something in common—we are pursuing life.
Not just an ordinary, getting-by kind of life. We want to make
our life count. We want to make the most of it. We want to
excel, expand, do better, leave an impact, experience the best,
the richness of all life has to offer—don't we?

Of course, we do, and if we are honest with ourselves, we
want abundance. Who doesn't want an abundant life! We all

have only one life to live, and we want to make it the best it can be, right? However, life is not abundant for most of us. In fact, it's minimal, marginal, ordinary, or basic at best. We may even feel we are just surviving. Why is that?

It's my goal to answer that question and help identify how we can turn things around to discover and live an abundant life.

THE PROMISE OF ABUNDANT LIVING

I want you to notice the words Jesus speaks in this scripture verse, **"The thief cometh not, but for to steal, and to kill, and to destroy: I am come that they might have life, and that they might have it more abundantly."** (John 10:10)

This verse promises we can have life, but more than that, it promises us an abundant life. To make this verse a realization in our life, we must understand a few things. Comprehending these basic things will assist us in acquiring and experiencing that abundant life.

Did you notice in that verse Jesus said, "I am come?" There is a reason he uses this phrase rather than just saying we can have an abundant life. He is laying the foundation for an abundant life, and he is stating his purpose. The whole reason he arrived on the planet is to bring us something—*life!* Not just an ordinary, everyday kind of life, but an *abundant* one at that!

If we believe Jesus's statement, then questions begin bubbling up in our hearts and minds and sometimes even come oozing out of our lips, such as:

What is life?
What does abundance mean?

How can I obtain it for myself?

Do I just get it when I believe or accept Jesus?

Is there anything I need to do to grab hold of it?

How will I know when I've got it?

And there are many, many more questions just begging to be answered.

However, many of us have heard these words of Jesus and initially felt the hope of their impact, but due to a lack of understanding, lost touch with them, and just let them settle into the recesses of our mind—assuming they must either be non-relevant, specific to salvation only, or too simplistic to really mean much of anything.

The first time we read these words as a new believer something stirs inside us and says, "Hey, I want that!" We strive to do better and be better, but because we're not confident in what better is, or because we don't know what it takes to obtain this abundant life or how it all connects, we tend to lose the grip of these words over time and so they lose their meaning.

I am here to tell you these words are more than all of that— they are inspiring! They are packed with promise, and they are still true today, almost 2,000 years after Jesus spoke them. I am here to answer most of the questions that are conjured up because of these words. So, let's dive in!

A PROMISE MADE IS A PROMISE KEPT

As I mentioned, these words of Jesus are a promise to us that we can have an abundant life. So, the first question we must answer is what is a promise? Well, according to the dictionary, a *promise* is "a declaration or an assurance that one will do a particular thing, or that a particular thing will happen."[1] In this case abundant life is a given. From God's perspective, abundant life is a certainty because he's made it available. It will happen. Jesus declared it, so indeed it will come to pass—or will it?

What most forget is that a promise is conditional—it goes two ways. For some reason when it comes to the promises of God, we tend to think since God said it, he will do it, but that's not necessarily true. Since promises are two-way streets, it means God will only do his part—*if*—we will do our part. Also keep this in mind, God has never ever broken his side of a promise. Human beings on the other hand...well that's another story altogether.

When we latch on to the words "abundant life," we comfort ourselves with them—we recite them over and over because something deep down inside ourselves understands they are true. As I said, they will come to pass and so we assume they will do so without much effort or thought on our part. We may say to ourselves, "Jesus has come to give me an abundant life." However, we miss the qualifying word he uses in the sentence. Jesus interjected the word "might." "They *might* have life" AND "they *might* have it more abundantly." Availability of an abundant life rests upon God and he has fulfilled his part, but the responsibility for attainment of an abundant life rests upon us. Have we fulfilled our part?

Notice, too, Jesus used a conjunction between the phrases which is why I capitalized it. Understand the word "and" not only connects the phrases, but it also marks a distinction between the two ideas. In other words, these phrases can stand alone. First, you can have life. If all you want is to just get by and receive what Jesus offers, then that's fine—that's what you will get. The gift of eternal life, after passing through this one, is quite an incredible gift. You can settle in and be ok with that—and most are, as you can see all around you.

And this is the record, that God hath given to us eternal life, and this life is in his Son. He that hath the Son hath life; and he that hath not the Son of God hath not life. (1 John 5:11-12)

However, a select few will realize the conjunction is also an invitation to *more* in the here and now. You can have more than just surviving. You can have more while living out this life, before reaching eternity. You can have abundance in this life, but it will be completely up to you. Of course, you cannot have abundance without first having the life Jesus offers up front. They go together, life and abundance. It's kind of like the old children's chant, "first comes love, then comes marriage," but in this case we could say first comes life, then comes abundance. Only after discovering the life Jesus offers can you also have the abundance mentioned. But there is a requirement involved here based upon the phrasing Jesus used.

Abundant life is conditional, meaning it's based on something. On what is it based? We are given some insight in the qualifying word we've already identified—might. To figure this out and gain understanding, we need to learn a few more things about this scripture verse.

Since the New Testament was written in Greek, the word translated "life" in the Greek, is the word *zōē* (pronounced dzo-ay') which carries the meaning of "not only life but vitality, animate, of the absolute fullness both essential and ethical, a life active and vigorous, devoted to God and blessed."[2]

And the Greek word for "abundant" is *perissos* (pronounced per-is-sos') and means "abundant, more, beyond measure, advantage, over and above, more than is necessary, something further, superior, extraordinary, surpassing, or uncommon."[3]

When we put these two together, we get a better understanding of what Jesus is telling us. We can have an uncommon, active life that is consistently growing and becoming more than we ever thought it could be. In other words, there is no limit to how this life can unfold and be fulfilling for us—or is there?

UNDERSTANDING OUR LIMITATIONS

Unfortunately, there is a limit placed on the abundance we can receive and achieve, but it's not a limit placed by God. Although he used a qualifying word in the scripture (might), he did not place that qualifier upon himself. Rather, he placed that qualifier upon us (*they* might).

We can limit our abundant life because it's based upon us and the exercise of our might. If we want an abundant, overflowing life then we must exercise our might to achieve it.

Before God was in our lives, there was an even greater limitation. Without God and the arrival of Jesus on the scene, an abundant life was not even possible. It was totally out of the question. This is why Jesus said, "I am come." He came to remove that limitation so an abundant life would now be possible—not guaranteed—but at least possible because he removed the greatest barrier to its access.

To understand how he did that and the greatest limitation, we must understand what he brought with him when he came.

Obviously, we see in scripture that he brought salvation to our spiritual lives. Because of mankind's sin, there was no option for an abundant life. Sin is a destroyer—it tears down and kills. There is no life in sin. We are told that in the beginning of John 10:10. Remember how the verse began, "The thief cometh not, but for to steal, and to kill, and to destroy." The thief in this case is sin. How do we know this?

EVEN GOD BREATHES

We must go back to the creation story in the Bible's book of Genesis. We read in Genesis 2:7, **"And the Lord God formed man of the dust of the ground, and breathed into his nostrils the breath of life; and man became a living soul."**

When you read all the verses prior to this one (Go ahead and do it now since it's not that long. You can come back to this spot when you're done.), you learn God created everything that exists in our world. This verse provides a flashback to the specifics of man's creation, and we see that although man was alive physically because he was created ("formed") by God, he didn't become a "living soul" until God breathed into him the "breath of life."

The word "breath" is *nᵉšāmâ* (pronounced nesh-aw-maw') in Hebrew (the Old Testament was written mostly in Hebrew) and means "breath, wind, and spirit."[4] If we understand God is a Spirit according to John 4:24 (**"*God is a Spirit:* and they that worship him must worship him in spirit and in truth."** Emphasis mine), then we can see that God put a part of himself into man when he created him, and that's how man became a living soul. Without God within, the man had no soul. Hence, man's origin or source of life is directly tied to his relationship with God.

A short while later in Genesis we see man lost this God-placed Spirit within due to sin when he disobeyed God and ate of the forbidden tree. We read that the serpent (a reference to the devil—Revelation 12:9 **"And the great dragon was cast out, *that old serpent, called the Devil*, and Satan, which deceiveth the whole world: he was cast out into the earth, and his angels were cast out with him."** Emphasis mine) tricked mankind into sinning against God and stole the life right out of them. Because of their sin, God drove man out of the Garden of Eden and more importantly, from God's presence. And so, God took back his Spirit that had been placed in man, since God's Holy Spirit cannot dwell with sin. The access door to abundant living was slammed shut.

Therefore, the entrance to this life had to be restored and the door reopened, which was the entire mission of Jesus in a nutshell. Perhaps this is why Jesus said, **"I am the door: by me if any man enter in, he shall be saved, and shall go in and out, and find pasture."** (John 10:9) So now we understand why Jesus said, "I am come that they might have life." If Jesus hadn't fulfilled his mission and restored availability to this life, we would remain stuck in sin—unable to experience abundance as promised. Now we can have confidence knowing the necessary access exists, but the rest is up to us. If we exercise our might we can obtain the promise.

WHAT IS ABUNDANCE?

Let's define abundance. What is it and why is it important? I know we explored abundance from the Greek definition previously, but now I'm asking, *what is abundance to you*? The dictionary says *abundance* simply means "a very large quantity of something."[5] With this broad meaning, it can be hard to define abundance because what it means in my life may be different than how you define it in your own life. What I consider large may be deemed small in your eyes or vice versa.

Now, let's not make the mistake of assuming abundance equals happiness. What do I mean by that? Anytime we have a little of something and assume if we had just a little more, it would make us happy, we are equating that happiness with abundance. This is so far from the truth! However, the enemy uses this thought to deceive us and keep us from experiencing true abundance.

This thought is also self-defeating. Once we attain whatever we pursue, we may experience momentary happiness but when that brief happiness fades or wears off (and it will because happiness is a feeling, which is an emotion and emotions are based on our thoughts, and our thoughts change over time and our circumstances), we wonder, *why am I no longer happy with what I obtained?* We conclude that we miscalculated how much we needed to be happy. So, we recalculate and think, *I must need more of this something than I thought I did,* and we strive to obtain even more, and the cycle goes on and on.

To experience true abundance, we must define it for ourselves by asking how much is enough for me? We must ask this of ourselves in every area of our life. How much money is enough for me to live? How much energy do my spouse and kids require of me? How much brain power do I have to expend for the kind of work I perform? How strong are my relationships? And the list continues. These are not easy questions and because they are not easy, we may instead slip into the happiness mode and ask ourselves simpler questions. Am I happy with my finances?

Am I happy in my marriage? Am I happy with my physical health? Am I happy with my social life?

While these types of questions may provide temporary feedback and minor clues regarding our happiness level, they do not reveal much about abundance in our lives. Rather, they may indicate where we need to refocus or reallocate our energies. Simply recognizing we're not happy with our finances doesn't answer the question if we have abundance with our finances. We might instead be dealing with a bigger issue in our lives like greed or lust that needs to be addressed first. If we're unhappy with our finances because we've been eyeing up that fancy sports car or new house we desire and we don't have enough to purchase it, it may not be an abundance issue after all.

HAPPINESS VERSUS CONTENTMENT

If we look up the definition of the word *happy* in the dictionary it says it's "feeling or showing pleasure or contentment."[6] We tend to focus on the feeling of pleasure rather than contentment as happiness. But if we focused on contentment, we would find much more satisfaction with our lives. In my example of the sports car, when we focus on contentment instead of happiness, we may realize that our current vehicle is meeting our needs and that others wish they had the car we have—or even had one at all. It starts to put things in proper perspective. With that adjusted perspective, we begin to see we have enough, and our craving is something more like greed. There is nothing wrong with having a sports car, but we must examine our motivations as to why we want it. If it is clouding our perspective, then we must face the truth and adjust our expectations. When we have the correct perspective, we may see we have abundance already because our current car might be the very tool we can use to take a neighbor without a car to church or grocery shopping.

I believe we all need to adopt Paul's outlook when he wrote, **"Not that I speak in respect of want: for I have learned, in whatsoever state I am, therewith to be content. I know both how to be abased, and I know how to abound: every where and in all things I am instructed both to be full and to be hungry, both to abound and to suffer need. I can do all things through Christ which strengtheneth me."** (Philippians 4:11–13)

Based on this scripture, we can conclude we are able to learn to become content. It takes time and effort to learn something. We must practice a skill to possess it. Therefore, we can learn to restrain our wants and desires and be satisfied with our current state. In so doing, we can create abundance for ourselves. Perhaps you can also be encouraged by Paul's words in 1 Timothy 6:6, **"But godliness with contentment is great gain."**

When we reach this level or place of contentment and begin to see we have abundance, is that good or bad? In other words, is abundance inherently good or evil? Will abundance lead us down one road or the other by simply having it? Will I be encouraged to help others by using my abundance, or will I become preoccupied with losing it and want to hoard it?

I believe abundance is neutral and the resulting road we travel is determined by the state of our heart. That is why we must define abundance first and foremost for ourselves in the context of our contentment. By determining with what level we will be content, we can then determine what we want to do with our abundance.

This is not an easy consideration, and it evolves as we learn more about abundance and ourselves. My current level of contentment could change tomorrow as time and circumstances change. For most, we may find contentment is easier to achieve the older we get. We find the importance we placed on certain things early on wanes as other things take their place. For example, right out of college it was important for me to be successful in my career, but when I had a family, I found my family became much more important to me than my career, and I was willing to sacrifice work hours for more family time.

ABUNDANCE—NOW WHAT?

Once we can define abundance in our lives, then we must question what to do with it. I believe the purpose of abundance is to share it and bless others with it. If we only grasp the abundance, we become greedy and stingy, and it hardens our heart. We learn a great lesson from a story Jesus told in the Bible:

> And he said unto them, "Take heed, and beware of covetousness: for a man's life consisteth not in the abundance of the things which he possesseth." And he spake a parable unto them, saying, "The ground of a certain rich man brought forth plentifully: And he thought within himself, saying, What shall I do, because I have no room where to bestow my fruits? And he said, This will I do: I will pull down my barns, and build greater; and there will I bestow all my fruits and my goods. And I will say to my soul, Soul, thou hast much goods laid up for many years; take thine ease, eat, drink, and be merry. But God said unto him, Thou fool, this night thy soul shall be required of thee: then whose shall those things be, which thou hast provided?

So is he that layeth up treasure for himself, and is not rich toward God." (Luke 12:15–21)

I hope it captured your attention when Jesus said, "for a man's life consisteth not in the abundance of the things which he possesseth." We learn having abundance does not provide us life, but it's what we do with our abundance that enhances or even provides us life. Many have the process backward. They spend their life pursing what they consider abundance but end up empty and living a life without meaning. However, those pursuing true abundance for the purpose of helping others find themselves fulfilled, content, and overly satisfied.

I hope this scripture also revealed that it's not the attainment of abundance that makes a difference. And while it's good to share that abundance with others, it's also not the purpose of attaining it. I know on the surface that can be a little confusing, but please stick with me here. If life is not found in the mere attainment of abundance and life is not fully experienced in sharing abundance with others, then where does life occur in the process? That's just it—life occurs in the process itself! In other words, life is in the journey. This seems a bit cliché, and that's why I didn't just come right out and say it that way earlier. I wanted you to reach the same conclusion on your own so it would hold more meaning.

ABUNDANCE IS A JOURNEY

How does this scripture prove life occurs in the journey? Because of the way the story ends. Reread the last phrase, "and is not rich toward God." This is our clue. If life was found in the accumulation of abundance, the man in the story would not have been called a "fool" since he would have accomplished the purpose. If life was found in sharing the abundance with others, then the story would have ended something like this instead, "and is not rich toward others." However, the story didn't even mention others, so that can't be where life is found either. Why then does the story end with the rebuke that this man should have been rich toward God?

When we are rich toward God, our abundance is offered back to God, who originally supplied it. We show we are open to doing with our abundance whatever he directs. When we are rich toward God, it means God's desires become our desires. One of God's main desires is that we help others, which is a way we show them love. God is love according to scripture (see 1 John 4:8).

God's main desire is that we would have a deep, meaningful relationship with him. This is God's first priority—that we are in an intimate relationship with him. We all understand intimacy takes time. It's a journey. Therefore, true abundance is a result of this intimacy journey.

How can I confirm this again scripturally? Let's look at Matthew 7:21–23: **"Not every one that saith unto me, Lord, Lord, shall enter into the kingdom of heaven; but he that doeth the will of my Father which is in heaven. Many will say to me in that day, Lord, Lord, have we not prophesied in thy name? and in thy name have cast out devils? and in thy name done many wonderful works? And then will I profess unto them, *I never knew you*: depart from me, ye that work iniquity."** (Emphasis mine.)

We see in this passage that those talking to the Lord knew who he was, understood what he wanted them to do, and did it—but Jesus's response was, "I never knew you." The word "knew" in the Greek is *ginōskō* (pronounced ghin-oce'-ko) and means "to know, perceive, or understand."[7] However, this word also carries with it the connotation of sexual intercourse between a man and a woman.

We all know sexual intercourse cannot happen unless there is a baring of all or an exposing of everything that is usually hidden or covered up. Jesus's use of this word indicates those in this story did not bare everything to him, expose everything to him, or show him who they really were.

Taking this further, God knows everything about us already, so why would he be upset they didn't reveal everything to him that he already knows? The only answer must be that it isn't important for him to know, but rather it must be important for us to know ourselves. To really know ourselves—honestly, as raw, as naked, as exposed as possible. To have no hidden agendas, no lies we buy into, nothing we coverup and ignore about ourselves.

The only way to truly know ourselves is through the process of time and experiences—when we face up to who we are in each moment and through every mistake made. As we journey through life, we have experiences that help us discover who we are by how we choose to react and whether we will learn, grow, and adjust because of those experiences and reactions. Therefore, I conclude that true life comes by pursing abundance and having the correct purpose for that pursuit is of utmost importance.

It is my goal to show you how to get this process correct in your life so you too can enhance your purpose and find joy in the abundance God provides. To do that we must understand it will take exercise and exercise is work. Like exercise at the gym, if we simply try all the different machines and lift various weights without any program, methodology, or reason, we tire ourselves, gain nothing, and may not want to do it again. On the other hand, if we go to the gym with a plan in mind to focus on our core for example and do exercises pinpointing that area, we'll still get tired, but also feel a sense of accomplishment that we are a step closer to our goal. That's what I hope the following chapters do for you. Provide you a methodology on which to focus and help you understand how you can create abundance in each area of your life.

TAKE AWAYS

- Jesus promises us not only the availability of life in eternity but that we can experience abundance in our earthy living in as found in John 10:10.

- A *promise* is "a declaration or an assurance that one will do a particular thing, or that a particular thing will happen." But we also know it's a two-way street. God will always do his part, but to see fulfillment of this promise, we must do what he asks of us—that is our part.

- From God's perspective, life and abundance go together and are in sequence. We first are invited into life through Christ and then we are given access to true abundance.

- The only limitation in receiving abundance is placed upon us. We must exercise our might to pursue the abundance God has in store for us.

- The thief of abundance is sin. We must confess our sin and repent, that is turn away from our sin and turn toward God. Placing our trust and reliance upon him helps get us on the pathway to life and abundance.

- Abundance is not necessarily associated with our happiness because happiness is an emotion that can change over time and is tied to our circumstances. Abundance is associated with our contentment and contentment starts with honestly questioning ourselves and our motives. The most important question we should ask is, "How much is enough?"

- Abundance is neutral, it's what we do with it that can have a negative or positive impact on us and others. It can either bring life or destroy it.

- Abundance is a journey and life occurs in the process.

NEXT STEPS

Take some time to reflect on your life. Have you ever asked yourself the hard questions? Questions like: How much is enough in every area of my life? Am I chasing down happiness rather than contentment? Has sin in my life been stealing away my opportunities for abundance? These questions will require brutal honesty to reveal significant answers and they will take time to evaluate. So, find a quiet place, set aside a good chunk of time, and really dig in. If you are struggling with the answers, especially the one regarding sin in your life, simply ask God to forgive and help you. He's waiting for your communication, and he longs for a meaningful relationship where you can be intimate and real with him.

TRANSITION

In the next chapter we are going to learn what it means to exercise our M.I.G.H.T. We know Jesus left the responsibility for attaining abundance upon our shoulders, when he used the qualifier "they might" in John 10:10. Therefore, we need to know what he was implying for us to be successful in our responsibility. Find out by joining me in the next chapter.

3
DEFINING YOUR M.I.G.H.T.

*"Potential means nothing if you
don't do anything with it."*
–ANONYMOUS

WHAT DO YOU THINK of when you hear or read the word might? It carries two connotations with it. You either think of strength or of possibility, depending on how it's used. In reality, it is both! I'm going to stretch your thinking by saying might is the possibility of strength.

You see, even strength isn't strength until it's exercised. What do I mean by this? My son and I like to lift weights to stay in shape and build muscle. The heavier the weights we lift, the bigger the muscles we eventually develop. However, while I know my son is strong because he's got big bulging biceps, those biceps only hold the possibility of strength. Until the bar is loaded with weights and until he grasps the bar to lift it, there is no evident strength, only the possibility of it. Once he lifts the bar and begins to move it his strength becomes realized and evident.

Why does this matter? Because when Jesus says we can have an abundant life, that it's dependent upon us and our might, he is saying there is great possibility and resulting strength that can be developed by exercising certain things which result in an abundant life.

However, nothing in this life stays stationary. Things are always moving forward—that's the way time works. Except for two miraculous instances noted in the Bible, time only moves forward. Because we must live this life confined by time, everything that touches this life is also touched by time and therefore is moving forward along with us.

Taking my example further, my son can't go to the gym one day and expect to come out of the gym after his workout completely buff, no matter how much he wishes. He must continue to exercise to build those muscles. Day after day he must visit the gym and lift the weights, and only then will the muscles he desires begin to develop. Not only that, he must also steadily increase those weights, if he desires those muscles to get even bigger. Should he take a few weeks off from going to the gym, he'll find those muscles he previously developed will reduce in size. And, if he stops all his activity, then eventually he will lose the muscle tone and flexibility he once had.

That is why we must exercise our might to not only obtain an abundant life, but to maintain it and increase its abundance. *Exercise* according to the dictionary is described as "a process or activity carried out for a specific purpose, especially one concerned with a specified area or skill."[1] However, I like the simpler definition that states exercise is "to use or to apply."

So, if we are to use or apply our might, then the question arises on what or how? Obviously, the resulting answer is on the right things, at the right times.

Continuing my example, if my son doesn't lift weights to build muscles but rather stands and pushes against a wall, some muscle will develop by the resistance the wall offers, but it will not be nearly the same as lifting weights. Also, if he works all day and wears himself out, then attempts to lift weights without any energy left, he will be at a deficit to lift the proper weight and his muscles won't benefit. Lastly, if my son is not ready or capable of lifting 300 pounds, then he must begin with a weight he is capable of lifting and increase the weight over time. It's got to be the right things at the right times!

WHAT IS LIFE

So now the question arises, what is life? Of course, we can simply think of life as the means of breathing in and out. Being alive physically can be considered life. However, we've previously established that there's more to this life than that. We all understand that life on this earth encompasses several areas. In my analysis of my own life for well over half a century, I determined life is made up of the following components:

Mental State
Emotional State
Relationships
Social Connections
Spiritual Core
Physical Existence
Financial State

Some may want to interject and say that I'm missing various areas or components like work life, recreational life, or some other aspects of life. But I ask that you pause and consider those examples are simply complex combinations of the areas I have already identified. For instance, your work life is a combination of your mental state and physical existence (depending on the type of work you do) as well as your social connections (since most of us work with other people) and financial state (since most of us also work to get paid). Let's consider your recreational life. Isn't it a combination of your emotional state (you relax and participate in recreation because of how it makes you feel), your physical existence (since recreation either requires our physical movement or the lack thereof), and your social connections (since we tend to participate in recreation with others to whom we are aligned)?

When you attempt to break life down into only the essential areas, I believe you will reach the same conclusion I have—that there are only seven major areas as identified here. These seven areas comprise our complete life like spokes in a wheel. They work together. You can't just focus on one area without it affecting the other areas.

For example, if you focus only on your financial state and devote your time to only working to make a lot of money, you must realize you are perhaps endangering if not damaging your physical existence by not getting the proper physical exercise or enough movement in your life—especially if you have a desk job. You may also be hurting your relationships because you're trading worktime for being with your spouse and children. You may also be eroding your mental and emotional states because if your work is very taxing you may be pushing emotions out of the way and straining your mental capacity by focusing on only one train of thought.

You see it's all connected. Even if you flip the example to another area and say you only focus on your spiritual life, you may become, as some would say, "so heavenly minded that you're no earthly good." You lose touch with the ability to relate to the people around you and so your relationships are frayed. Or you haven't focused on making any money as you've studied God's word, so your financial state is falling apart. Or you've shut yourself up in your prayer closet and dropped the ball with communicating with your friends, so your social circle has been broken. So, I'll say it again—it's all connected. And this is the way God intended it to be.

When we think of having an abundant life, we must think in terms of having it in every area of our life. In fact, when God references an abundant life, this is what he means. He's including every area of our life in his promise. Unfortunately, many think only in terms of one area and usually that is in the realm of their finances.

Using my wheel analogy again, if you think of a wheel with spokes and one of those spokes is broken, you now have a weak point within the wheel. If the wheel hits a bump or a sharp object at that weak point, it could affect the whole wheel. The wheel can get a flat or get warped and the other spokes can even get broken as a result. I know what you're going to say here, that I'm talking about balance. But it's more than that, it's understanding how each one impacts the other and how the center hub influences and strengthens the spokes.

That's why we also must have the proper hub in the center of that wheel with all the spokes connected, and then the entire wheel will rotate in relationship to the hub. In other words, we could say it is the hub that will stabilize the spokes and regulate the rotation of the wheel—its speed, its angle, and its performance.

It's interesting to note that in Ezekiel chapter one, the prophet describes his vision—an encounter with heavenly spiritual beings—and he gives a very detailed description of their appearance. As part of that description, he points out in verse 16 that these spiritual beings included "a wheel in the middle of a wheel." This sounds a lot like a wheel, spoke, and hub design to me—especially considering that he states that "the spirit of the living creature was in the wheel." In other words, the spirit was in the hub or core of the wheel.

Ezekiel can be difficult to read and understand because the prophet is describing something he never saw before and something we've most likely never seen either. We have no reference to comprehend and compare it to. Here are the specific verses for you:

> **The appearance of the wheels and their work was like unto the colour of a beryl: and they four had one likeness: and their appearance and their work was** *as it were a wheel in the middle of a wheel.* **When they went, they went upon their four sides: and they turned not when they went. As for their rings, they were so high that they were dreadful; and their rings were full of eyes round about them four. And when the living creatures went, the wheels went by them: and when the living creatures were lifted up from the earth, the wheels were lifted up. Whithersoever the spirit was to go, they went, thither was their spirit to go; and the wheels were lifted up over against them:** *for the spirit of the living creature was in the wheels.* (Ezekiel 1:16–20 Emphasis mine.)

You've probably already figured out what I'm going to say next. Before we identify the correct hub for our wheel, we must identify the wheel itself. The wheel is you. It's your life—the sum of every experience you've had. It's the sum of you or in other words, your soul. It's the record of who you are. You have the ability to make decisions and take actions and it's these decisions and actions that propel you down the path of life. Each decision you make can turn your life in a new direction and every action results in a road to travel.

Just like a wheel has tread to help it grip and move forward, you have potential. Everything you have experienced will propel you forward toward some new territory or destination. A new path always lies before you—it's a matter of how you allow your experiences to connect you to that path and move you along it. At times the difficulties, struggles, and hardships in your life wore down the tread and you lost momentum. However, the cool thing about our wheel comparison is that you can get a retreaded tire simply by allowing your perspective to shift. A retread is when fresh tread is overlaid on top of the worn tread giving the tire new life and added potential. Seeing things in a different way and learning as you go, will allow you to gain fresh potential as you implement what you've learned.

Now let's discuss the hub. In my opinion the center of the wheel keeping everything else in balance is God or our spiritual life. I'll go back to our main scripture verse of John 10:10 when Jesus said, "*I am come.*" As I pointed out previously, it was only by Jesus coming and redeeming us from our sin that we could have access to an abundant life. Without God's redemption, true life and abundance were not even possible. Therefore, I believe a relationship with God must be the center of our properly balanced wheel or the main hub from which abundance can be experienced for all areas of our lives.

YOUR M.I.G.H.T.

Before I start addressing each area of our lives and outlining how we can obtain abundance, let's first understand what it means to have *might* in the context of what I am addressing. In this case I'm using the word might as a mnemonic, which is a device for remembering the life areas we need to exercise to obtain the abundance we desire. So, you can think of M.I.G.H.T. this way.

Mental
Interactions
God
Health
Treasury

Now, right away you will notice there are only five areas listed here in the word *might* versus the seven components we identified previously for the areas that compose our entire life. I combined the two missing components with the ones identified in this list of five, as five is easier to remember than seven and they work in conjunction with this word might. I really want us to focus on this word, since it is repeated in our foundational scripture in John 10:10. That way you won't forget the scripture, its conditional component, and the meaning of the word *might*, as well as the areas of our lives for which it stands.

As we progress, we will discuss each section of our mnemonic separately, but for now let's expand it a bit so you can see that all seven components of our lives are truly covered in this five-letter word.

While the M in M.I.G.H.T. stands for Mental in our mnemonic device, it will also stand for our emotional state. This is because our emotions stem or arise from what we think. In other words, our emotions do not stand alone. They are generated from our mental facilities. In the group of seven components our emotional state is a stand-alone category because our emotions can impact the other areas of our lives to a large degree apart from our other mental capacities. What do I mean by this? Since the connection between the mental and emotional is a deep and almost hidden one (most of us don't realize there is a connection that can be controlled), it may not seem sensible that we can feel a certain way. We may try to rationalize away the feelings through our mental capacities. I will dig deeper into this later but let's say for now that due to prolonged mental thoughts over time, emotions can become so ingrained in us that they seem to be naturally occurring and have a life of their own. Sometimes we must deal with this area of our lives separately. For now, though, we will address the emotional with the mental and count them as one area.

The I in M.I.G.H.T. stands for Interactions, which is a reference to both the relational and social arenas of our lives. Some will argue you can have an interaction with an inanimate object like a stapler but that is only a one-sided interaction, which by definition does not measure up. I can use the stapler to fasten some papers together and once used the interaction is over and complete, but it was all a one-sided interaction in the sense that I was the one who forced the operation of the stapler upon the paper. To have a genuine interaction there must be an action that occurs as two or more participants affect one another. This can only meaningfully occur in human interactions. If I wanted a true interaction with the stapler, the stapler would or should have the opportunity to respond to my forcing the staple through the paper by choosing not to or varying where on the paper or how many staples to use or what kind of staples, etc. This is why I have chosen to represent our relationships through the choice of the word interactions.

It's only through our human interactions that we establish, maintain, and grow our relationships.

Social interactions are only larger scale or broader relationships. Typically, they may not be as deep or as meaningful as our personal relationships, but they are still human interactions and so I will address the social area of our lives within the realm of our relationships. Social interactions have a certain uniqueness that is handled differently than intimate relationships and they can be considered a separate component overall, but for sake of our review, we will address social and relational aspects together.

The G in M.I.G.H.T. stands for God who is the center of our spiritual lives. Quite coincidentally the G is in the center of the word *might*—but then again, knowing a little bit about how God works, it's probably not so coincidental after all. I believe this also lends credence to my previous statement that our spiritual lives must be the center or hub of our wheel.

The H in M.I.G.H.T. stands for our Health. For most of us when we think about our health we tend to think in terms of our physical being. Although health can be measured in the other areas of our lives (i.e., our mental and emotional health would be part of our mental life, our financial health would be a part of our financial life, etc.), for now it will only apply to our physical existence.

Lastly, the T in M.I.G.H.T. stands for Treasury or in other words, our finances.

So, there we have it! In this short five letter word we find the grace of God to cover our entire existence. M=Mental (Mental and Emotional), I=Interactions (Relational and Social), G=God

(Spiritual), H=Health (Physical), and T=Treasury (Financial). I purposefully used the word grace here for a reason because the number five throughout scripture references God's grace. When we use this five-letter word M.I.G.H.T., we also find buried within it a grace that God provides us to make up for our short falls.

As we move forward let's continue with our wheel analogy, and as we outline what abundance means in each area of our lives let's start with the hub of the wheel, or in other words what lies in the center and from which everything else branches outward. Also remember as we move forward to experience God's abundance in each area of our lives that it's going to take exercise, and exercise is work. It will be hard at times, and we will have to learn to be focused, determined, and disciplined if we want to experience the results and rewards of God's abundant life.

Exercise must become a way of life. Like building physical muscles adheres to a use-it-or-lose-it natural law, it's the same way when it comes to building spiritual muscles. You can't say yes to God today and no tomorrow, still expecting an abundant life to continue. Only God knows the heart of man, and he offers grace so the well of abundance may not dry up over-night. Eventually without the proper care and maintenance of God's word in our heart, the abundance we've experienced may become only a memory.

TAKE AWAYS

- Might is only the possibility of strength because strength isn't strength until it's exercised. It's in the exercise or actual movement that we begin to reveal our true potential.

- The thing we call life on this earth is comprised of seven components: our mental state, emotional state, relationships, social connections, spiritual core, physical existence, and financial state.

- These components are like spokes in a wheel stabilized by a hub or a core. They rotate together. You can't just focus on one area without it affecting the other areas. It's more than balance; it's an understanding of how each one impacts the other and how the center hub influences and strengthens the spokes.

- The wheel represents your life. Your potential lies within, and it depends on what you do with your life—the decisions and actions you take that will begin to display your potential. However, you can alter your potential through perspective changes. When you shift your perspective, you are able to go down unexplored roads previously unknown to you.

- The center of our wheel is a hub from which the spokes are held in place. It's where strength and stability come from for the spokes. The center of our lives must be a spiritual core as it's the place from which abundance for every area of our life will come.

- Our M.I.G.H.T. is a mnemonic device for us to be able to remember the areas we need to exercise our discipline and determination to obtain abundance. It stands for M=Mental (Mental and Emotional), I=Interactions

(Relational and Social), G=God (Spiritual), H=Health (Physical), and T=Treasury (Financial).

NEXT STEPS

Take time to reflect on some of your past decisions and actions. Just concentrate on the more meaningful life altering ones that have guided you to this point in your life. Were they made from a spiritual core or not? Can you identify the ones that resulted in positive changes and the ones that caused negative impacts? Did you recognize the ones you wish you could do over if given the chance?

You must realize all that is in the past and what really matters is what lies ahead. What decisions or actions will you put into motion to get you down more enjoyable roads? Even if life has been good and rosy for you, there is always a chance for improvement. Will you focus more on the development of your spiritual core and try to implement it to strengthen every other area of your life? Are you interested in abundance in all components that make up your life?

TRANSITION

If you have answered yes to those last few questions, then it's time to read the next chapter. If you're not ready yet, that's understandable—you may need to take some more time to reflect, pray, and ask God to help you let go of your past and its impact. You may need him to provide you a "retread" and help you with a perspective change—trust that he will. This book will still be here for you when you're ready and the next chapter will guide you in your journey.

4
YOUR SPIRITUAL CORE

*"All creatures are merely veils
under which God hides Himself."*
–Martin Luther

A T THE CENTER OF our existence, whether we acknowledge it
or not, is a spiritual core. I truly believe as Pierre Teilhard
de Chardin is alluded to as having said, "We are not human
beings having a spiritual experience; we are spiritual beings
having a human experience."[1] If the center of our being or
our wheel is the hub from which everything rotates, then
an abundant life can only come from having a spiritual
center. God must be within the core of who we are and what
we build our lives around for everything else to function
properly. This makes perfect sense when we consider that
God created us. We didn't decide to just show up on the
scene and shout, "Here we are world." Rather scripture tells
us that we were carefully and considerately made by God:
**"I will praise thee; for I am fearfully and wonderfully made:
marvellous are thy works; and that my soul knoweth
right well."** (Psalm 139:14)

If we don't believe in God, then it will be hard to even establish
a core. I am going to assume most of you believe in God or
you wouldn't be reading this book. However, I will take a few
moments to address when someone may not believe in God.
What becomes of their core?

A person's core without God can become almost anything else. Most of the time it becomes one of the areas we will be talking about, that is the physical, emotional, mental, financial, relational, or even something dubbed spiritual other than God. Of course, we know what happens to our wheel analogy when we replace our spiritual core with one of these other areas—our wheel becomes disproportioned and wobbly and can cause the other areas in our lives to become damaged and broken.

Some have a sense of spirituality but resist or refuse God. They try to fill their hub with something they call "spiritual" but is not truly the Creator of the universe. They make God in their own image instead of allowing God to make them into his image. For some that may mean witchcraft, hedonism, Buddhism, eastern mysticism, astrology, atheism, or some other variant. (Yes, I added atheism to this list. While atheists proclaim not to believe in God, by default they have made themselves the center of their universe, or you could say they have made themselves God, whether they admit it or not.) Having read about some of these and experienced a touch of them in my own life, I believe these encounters encourage focus on one area of life, claiming to provide satisfaction—but ultimately, we still end up with brokenness and dysfunction at the center of our lives.

FILLING THE CORE

We all sense our spiritual core and understand it's reserved for God. If we try to ignore it and avoid its proper filling, then something will fill it—usually self. Therefore, we become self-centered, focused on only pleasing ourselves. We may fake it by trying to say and do the right things to express concern for others, but when the heat is turned up in our lives, our true colors of selfishness will show. When we are alone and completely honest with ourselves, if we have acted this way, we feel regret and deep shame.

If we want true abundance and satisfaction deep in the center of who we are, then we must recognize and give God his proper place in our lives. To do that, we must first clean out the God space in our lives of the junk that has accumulated. We must make room for God in our lives. If we've allowed something other than God to reside in that space, we must let go, turn away from it and allow God to take up residence. Please don't misunderstand me, it's not about getting your life right before coming to God. It's about acknowledging God as the proper filler of that sacred space in our lives so he can come to us. We can think of it like this: it's like buying a brand-new car and planning to take proper care of it so it never sees a scratch, dent, or ding. However, once you get it home, you must park it in the driveway rather than the garage because the garage is packed full of boxes you haven't dealt with for years. You can't just pull the car into the garage because you will risk damaging items in the boxes, and you may scratch your car's beautiful paint. So, first you must look in the boxes, and then clean out the garage.

We call this first step of spiritual house-cleaning repentance. You must be willing to look at your life, point to the mess, and own it. Proverbs 28:13 says, **"He that covereth (*or hides*) his sins shall not prosper: but whoso confesseth and forsaketh them shall have mercy."** (Clarification mine.)

Please notice the "th" on the ends of the words covereth, confesseth, and forsaketh. In the King James Version of the Bible this little "th" implies a continuous action. So, you could read the words like this: continues to cover, continues to confess, and continues to forsake. This means that repentance is a continuous process. We don't just repent once, and we're done forever. Since we are humans and humans make mistakes, we need to periodically clean out the messes that accumulate. The sooner you do, the easier the job is. Don't let the devil tell you that you can't be forgiven when you just made a mistake because that's when you need it the most. You need to seek God's forgiveness and strength before the dust settles so you won't get buried under a mountain of stuff again.

I've made numerous messes in my life and cleaned one up only to discover I've made another one right behind me. Repentance isn't a one-time thing. It requires constant vigilance and attention. Each mistake brings us to a crossroads where we must make a fresh decision each time. Do we own up and admit our error, or do we try to hide it and avoid its reality? If we decide to hide it, our spiritual growth stops and even begins to decline until we make it right once more. Of course sincerity plays an enormous part of our repentance. We can't assume that when we've made a mistake that we can simply mutter a few words of apology to God and continue making the same mistake because in reality that's not a mistake at that point, it's a choice. When we get right with God, we turn on the tap for God to allow spiritual abundance to flow once again into our lives.

So, what does spiritual abundance look like? We'll dive further into scripture to discover the answer in a moment. However, I must also address the issue of the power of choice (or exercising our *might*).

THE POWER OF CHOICE

God gives us all the power of choice, whether we believe in him or not. It's another built-in mechanism of the human being.

We decide if we want to acknowledge God or not. You might ask why God put this feature into the structure of man. Why didn't he just make us all know about him and love him right from the start? Well, the answer is quite simple.

Creator God already made beings that knew and loved him because they were created that way—angels. The basic angel does not have the power of choice. They are beings who were solely created to serve God and they are only influenced by their leader or the archangel over them. God created archangels as heads or leaders over the different types or categories of basic angels. These archangels may be a cross or hybrid between how angels and men were designed, since they may have the power of choice—it's not entirely clear in scripture if they do or don't (I believe they do given the story of Lucifer and his decision to pursue his pride and make himself like God).

We know the basic angels are subjected to the influence of leadership, because we are told in scripture when Lucifer (one of the archangels) fell from heaven (and God's grace) that he took one-third of the basic angels with him. Is it just coincidence that there are three archangels named in scripture (Lucifer being one of them) and that one-third of the basic angels went with him? It's highly unlikely this would work out so precisely mathematically unless it was a result of leadership influence. Since their leader had the most influence over them, they bought into his cause and followed where he went. (Isn't that similar in our society? If you want to influence the crowd, influence their leader. But I'm getting off topic here—just read some leadership books by John Maxwell and you'll see what I mean about the impact of leadership.)

God wanted to experience genuine love and for that to happen choice must be involved. If someone has a choice to love you or not, when they choose to do so, you know their love is freely given and genuine. We have a choice to make—to love and follow God or not. He isn't going to make us. He showed his love for us when he hung upon a cross for our sins so we would know his love was free and genuine toward us. Now it's up to us.

For those who reject Him, there may not be much point reading further. But for those willing to exercise their power of choice and show they want to know more about God, I invite you to please continue with me.

NATURE ABHORS A VACUUM

If we can see our lives through the lens of a spiritual being rather than merely a human one, it changes the way we see everything. As physical beings, if we think we are seeking some sort of spiritual understanding or religious skill, then we limit ourselves and our growth—our ability to have abundance spiritually. However, if we alter our perspective and allow ourselves to experience a paradigm shift, thinking of ourselves in terms of spiritual beings impacted by all things in this physical human experience, then we open ourselves up to possibilities, exponential growth, and the resulting spiritual abundance.

Let's continue discussing the concept of a spiritual core. We each have one and we must properly establish and nurture it. There is a God shaped hole or as Blaise Pascal alluded to, a God shaped vacuum in the heart of every man. I like considering it as a vacuum, because as my favorite high school science teacher Mr. K. taught me, nature abhors a vacuum. If a vacuum exists, nature will do everything it can to fill it. You can see the truth of this in people's lives around you. We have all seen those who try to fill this God hole with power, drugs, sex, money, prestige, or a slew of other things but often they end up broken and craving more and more, or empty and frustrated.

This was certainly true in my life. I mentioned the physical and emotional abuse I encountered growing up, so by the time I hit my teenage years, I was searching to fill the vacuum with any form of love and acceptance I could find. This led me to numerous, meaningless relationships and one-night stands. I didn't recognize it then, but I tried getting what I needed through the physical intimacy God designed for only those who are married. I was temporarily satisfying my flesh through the physical pleasure of each encounter while hoping deep within me I would find the lasting satisfaction of love, compassion, and acceptance. It's funny how my attempts had the opposite effect on me. After each relationship, I felt more rejected, alone, and confused.

Having known and experienced a little something about God during my childhood, I started searching in a different way. I did my best to read my Bible on my own (even as a teenager), but nothing seemed to make sense. Being raised Catholic, I strived to do what many called the right Christian things: attend mass (every morning with my parents before going to high school each day) and participate in the rites and rituals, but still I knew I was failing and failing miserably. Everything I tried was surface issues; nothing sunk in to fill the core that was within me.

By the time I completed junior college and headed to Northern Illinois University, which was my first year away from home,

I was the most dejected, lonely, and empty I had ever been. That was the hardest year of my life since I had no friendship base in a new location. I was failing at school (something I had never experienced before), couldn't get into the degree program I desired, and couldn't pursue my passion of music due to no financial backing. I was deep in despair and depression, once again contemplating suicide. However, my experience from years ago with the "voice" still lingered with me and kept me from going over the edge.

I knew I needed a fresh start and a break from my past, so I transferred colleges and moved as far as I could get from home at the time—a five-hour drive away to the University of Wisconsin-Eau Claire. In my new environment, I began looking for a power to sustain or even change me. I was craving something bigger than myself. I was looking for a spiritual infilling of the vacuum.

Unfortunately, my first thoughts were to explore black magic and the occult. I heard and read some things growing up that stimulated my interest, so I went to the college library and began researching. I was amazed with the books and information I found, all within simple reach and easy access. So, I began reading and thinking about it.

Remember, I was in a brand-new environment where no one knew me, and I knew no one. I started making some friends as people reached out to me all the while keeping my exploration of black magic and the occult to myself. Finally, after a few months of research and reading, I felt fear come over me as I discovered blood rituals and sacrifices (I am extremely squeamish at the sight of blood). It was enough to shake me, so I began asking my new friends if they knew about any of these things. It was like opening flood gates—they began telling me things and sharing what they were deeply involved in, which was the same stuff I had been reading. It rocked my world and frightened me.

I realized that whatever you open yourself up to will gravitate toward you, just like a vacuum—flip the switch on the vacuum and things around it get sucked in.

Looking back, it was the grace of God that kept me from getting in too deep. I got rid of the books and stopped hanging with those friends, since I decided that stuff wasn't for me, but I still felt there must be something more. For the next several years I wandered, feeling very empty but still searching—just not finding anything I was seeking. At least I knew it had to be something spiritual, something bigger than me.

About four years later, when my wife and I started dating, the relationship forced us to deal with things from our past. We were committed to each other and decided we needed help, so we sought counseling and got into a Bible study taught by a friend. The moment we finished our first lesson, it was as if someone threw on a light switch in a dark room. Everything changed for me. I learned having the right spiritual core matters!

HOW DO YOU DEVELOP THE RIGHT SPIRITUAL CORE?

Hopefully you understand that developing the right spiritual core takes work and exercise. It doesn't just come to you. You must find it for yourself. Everyone has their own personal journey. However, many of us choose the wrong roads to explore, like me with black magic and the occult. We must choose the road of our Creator.

First, we must recognize that we did not create ourselves. As almost any addiction treatment program will advocate, there is a higher power that placed us here. We will call that our Creator. We must then ask ourselves if we are created, did our Creator just place us here and turn his back on us? I don't think so. As a human race, we don't have the tendency to do that (some do, and I experienced that by being put up for adoption). Generally, when we create something and place it into the world, we follow-up with it to be sure it is doing well and prospering. Take parenting for example—parents in general look out for and take care of their children. If this wasn't the case, then humans wouldn't have lasted very long. We would have died off quickly due to natural disasters and predators. Rather, we protect, we nurture, and we train our children to survive.

If we do that, don't you think our Creator would do that too? He does and this makes sense since scripture tells us we are made in his image, meaning we take after our Creator. We share the same traits like children take after their parents.

So God created man in his own image, in the image of God created he him; male and female created he them. (Genesis 1:27)

Like as a father pitieth his children, so the Lord pitieth them that fear (*respect*) him. (Psalm 103:13) (Clarification mine.)

Can a woman forget her sucking child, that she should not have compassion on the son of her womb? yea, they may forget, yet will I (*God*) not forget thee. (Isaiah 49:15) (Clarification mine.)

The next logical question after understanding we are made in God's image and that he watches over us is, does he instruct us? A parent wanting the best for their child begins teaching the child the things the parent knows. So, is this true of God? Does he teach us?

I will instruct thee and teach thee in the way which thou shalt go: I will guide thee with mine eye. (Psalm 32:8)

Based on this scripture, it appears God is interested in teaching us and keeping a watchful eye upon us as a good parent would. Therefore, if God teaches us, how has he chosen to do so? He gave us his word, his blueprint for life called the Bible. Someone has said the word Bible is an acronym that stands for **B**asic **I**nstructions **B**efore **L**eaving **E**arth. I think that is very fitting in the context of a spiritual being having a human experience because as such, we would need some set of instructions to follow before the experience ends.

When I debated if I could trust the Bible as the sole source for my spiritual instruction, I weighed the fact that it has been around for thousands of years and is still the bestselling book. I pondered the fact that its basic principles haven't changed during that time. (I could draw your attention to the Dead Sea Scrolls as one source of proof that it hasn't changed, but there are other books that do a good job of discussing that.) I discovered there are numerous archaeological, cosmological, literary, natural, and other overwhelming evidences that support the Bible. I could point them out here, but then I would be writing a different book and others have already done a better job of that (check out Lee Strobel's book *The Case for Christ*). Therefore I determined to make the Bible the center of my belief system, since I also learned that the main character loved me enough to die for me. I know of no other religious or belief system that can say the same.

The next thing I determined was that I needed to know it for myself. While I needed the input of others to help me understand some things, I was certain that I could decipher what God wanted to say to me through his word rather than solely depending on someone else who was likely searching as I was. Surprisingly, I found these thoughts were supported by scripture itself.

Study to shew *thyself* approved unto God, a workman that needeth not to be ashamed, rightly dividing the word of truth. (2 Timothy 2:15) (Emphasis mine.)

Work out *your own salvation* with fear and trembling. (Philippians 2:12) (Emphasis mine.)

Therefore, I dug into the Bible and started reading, studying, and analyzing it for myself in addition to participating in a Bible study.

NO CONFUSION

I found things that were contrary to what I was taught as a Catholic and I felt convicted to change and follow God's word, not man's word. My refrain became: Know it for yourself!

Therefore, no matter what you may read, even in this book, I want you to, no I urge you, compel you and even beg you to read the Bible for yourself. Ask questions. God's not afraid of questions, and there's not one he can't answer. Seek opinions, study, break it apart, look deeper than just the surface, and figure it out for yourself. It is possible because God didn't make any of it too hard. My favorite part of scripture has become 1 Corinthians 14:33 **"For God is not the author of confusion."** I rely upon this to remind myself that if I come across something about God that I don't understand, it means I haven't asked enough questions, or studied enough because God will always make his ways crystal clear to those who really want to know them.

Thy hands have made me and fashioned me: give me understanding, that I may learn thy commandments. (Psalm 119:73)

Through thy precepts I get understanding: therefore I hate every false way. (Psalm 119:104)

The entrance of thy words giveth light; it giveth understanding unto the simple. (Psalm 119:130)

Great is our Lord, and of great power: his understanding is infinite. (Psalm 147:5)

For the Lord giveth wisdom: out of his mouth cometh knowledge and understanding. (Proverbs 2:6)

Please understand that a core is something that is unchangeable. It is usually something that provides sustainability for other areas that are reliant upon it. For example, think of a fruit like a peach or nectarine (which are my favorites). There is a center where the seed resides, and from this center the nutrients go outward to the other parts of the fruit to ensure it is growing appropriately. The outer parts provide some protection to the core, meaning that when storms come, or little bugs eat away at the outside, the core remains intact and in return the core continues to supply what is necessary to the other parts to fight off the attacks.

When we determine to build our spiritual core around God and his instruction manual, we are building something that cannot be destroyed by the annoyances of life. It is something that brings strength to every other area of our lives. It is absolutely necessary God is at the center of who we are if we want the other parts of our lives to thrive and experience abundance.

IT'S UP TO YOU

If you haven't already, you must resolve to settle on God's word as your spiritual center not just your handbook. I say this because God and his word are inseparable—they are one and the same. **"In the beginning was the Word, and the Word was with God, and the *Word was God*."** (John 1:1 Emphasis mine.) *Resolve* means you "decide firmly on a course of action."[2] In other words, you may say to yourself like I did, "I'm going to follow God's word no matter what."

What happens when you come across something that rubs you the wrong way? What will you do then? It's your response that will determine if you indeed have resolve or not. To be settled firmly means you don't change directions mid-stream. Unless you know for certain that what you are holding onto doesn't work and you are grabbing something you know will, it makes no sense to change. For example, if you were on a boat and it started sinking, if you grabbed the anchor hoping it would save you, you'd be in a sorry state—and you would know it very quickly. But say as you were going down with the anchor, you saw a life vest floating up toward the top. It would make sense to let go of the anchor and grab the life vest. However, the reverse wouldn't be true. It would be ludicrous to exchange the life vest for the anchor in that situation.

Unfortunately, that's what many do. Some start with God's word and are sailing along great until they encounter something in his word that disturbs them and tips their boat over. Rather than cling to the life vest of the word and let God guide them to a better and more complete understanding, they let go of the sure thing and clutch the anchor of this world.

We are not going to fully understand everything about God on this side of heaven. We simply must learn to accept whatever his word has to say and then apply it to the best of our ability to our lives. Are we going to like it 100 percent of the time? No!

Those of you who are married will understand this point. You fell in love with your spouse, and you got married. Does that mean you love every little thing about your spouse? By all means, no! Perhaps you don't love their morning dragon breath or scratchy toenails in bed or the way they zone out when watching their favorite show. But there is so much more you do love about them that you are willing to live with the rest. It is the same with God. We may not appreciate every little detail, or we wish that some things could be different, but we understand that he is the Creator of all things, and he has the best in mind for us. He has provided for our spiritual salvation, so whatever else is necessary for us, we will live with it because the benefits are abundant!

TAKE AWAYS

- We all have a spiritual core—a place where God is meant to reside, but many fill this residence with other things and find their lives caving in on themselves because they were never meant to bear the weight.

- Nature abhors a vacuum. Something will fill our spiritual core either by our design or by default due to our lack of attention.

- To give God his proper place in our lives we must first "clean out our garage" through a process we call repentance. Repentance simply means that we truly apologize to God for our mistakes, and we turn ourselves in his direction to stop doing what we used to do and begin following him instead.

- Repentance isn't a one-time thing. We can and should repent anytime we mess up and as humans we mess up often. God understands. He helps us mess up less often as we grow in our relationship with him.

- God gave us the power of choice. We can choose to love him or not—it's up to us. If we choose to love him, we prove to God that our love is genuine through obedience to his word.

- Developing the right spiritual core takes work and self-discovery. We must be diligent in our pursuit of understanding God. God has not made it hard to know him, but he does expect some effort on our part before he reveals himself entirely to us. This is no different than any other relationship. We must strive to be vulnerable, ask questions, and stick with our commitment when things get tough.

NEXT STEPS

Search your heart and determine before going forward if you have resolved that no matter what else you encounter, if God said it, then you're going to live it. If you're honestly struggling with this, spend some time reflecting about the ways God has proven his word over the span of time through nature, science, archology, and history. Perhaps it would be good to do some research on these topics for yourself. Maybe it would also benefit you to talk to some well-grounded Christians and ask them about their personal experience and belief in the scriptures. Once you are ready to commit to God and his word, the abundance he has for you will begin to flow.

TRANSITION

In this chapter, I have only touched upon the topic of a spiritual core. In the next chapter we will discuss what it means to have God fill your core with his presence. When that happens, it is as the Bible puts it: **"joy unspeakable"** (1 Peter 1:8), meaning words can't do justice to describe the joy of being filled with God's Spirit.

5
MORE FOR YOUR
SPIRITUAL CORE

*"Many Christians have the mistaken notion that
eternal life begins when they die. But that is not
biblically accurate. Eternal life begins when we
are born again into the Kingdom of God."*
–DR. DAVID JEREMIAH

IF JESUS CAME TO give us life and we can't truly have it without
him, then shouldn't we ask ourselves what he had to say about
this life? How do we obtain it? When does it begin? Doesn't
life start at birth?

In the Gospel of John chapter three we read of an encounter
Jesus had with a Pharisee named Nicodemus. By the time they
had this discussion, the Pharisees were generally opposed to
Jesus and his message. Understanding this makes the conversation between Jesus and Nicodemus that much more impressive
and important.

> There was *a man of the Pharisees*, named Nicodemus,
> *a ruler of the Jews*: The same *came to Jesus by night*,
> and said unto him, Rabbi, we know that thou art a
> teacher come from God: for no man can do these mir-
> acles that thou doest, except God be with him. Jesus
> answered and said unto him, "Verily, verily, I say unto

thee, *Except a man be born again, he cannot see the kingdom of God.*" Nicodemus saith unto him, How can a man be born when he is old? can he enter the second time into his mother's womb, and be born? Jesus answered, "Verily, verily, I say unto thee, *Except a man be born of water and of the Spirit, he cannot enter into the kingdom of God.* That which is born of the flesh is flesh; and that which is born of the Spirit is spirit. Marvel not that I said unto thee, Ye must be born again. The wind bloweth where it listeth, and thou hearest the sound thereof, but canst not tell whence it cometh, and whither it goeth: so is every one that is born of the Spirit." Nicodemus answered and said unto him, How can these things be? (John 3:1–9 Emphasis mine.)

Nicodemus approached Jesus by night due to the underlying strife the Pharisees had with Jesus. Nicodemus took a big risk approaching him. Had he been discovered out in the open chatting with Jesus there would have been huge ramifications for Nicodemus. Perhaps he would have been ostracized and rejected from his place of power and position. We know Nicodemus was a well-respected and popular person because the gospel detail informs us he was a "ruler of the Jews," which most likely meant he was a part of the ruling council of the Sanhedrin, of which there were only seventy members. Think of it in terms of a senator in the US. To reach that level of power and position, Nicodemus must have had great knowledge of the Jewish Torah, as well as the laws of the land, and the concerns or issues of society and people of the day.

Talk about a risk! He believed what he thought about Jesus was important enough to talk over with him. If he was wrong, he would have lost everything he built in his life. I'm sure to reach that point of experience and insight he was no longer a young man, so he came to Jesus under the cover of darkness— hoping not to be spotted or recognized by those passing by.

The conversation began quite pleasantly and plainly, when Nicodemus basically said he thought he knew who Jesus was. He stated that even the Pharisees recognized no one could be performing the miracles Jesus was performing without having been sent from God.

However, Jesus quickly guided the conversation to something of utmost importance, which on the surface seemed quite strange. It would seem more natural for Jesus to acknowledge what Nicodemus just said and then proceed into some clarifying comments about who he was and his mission. But Jesus was not concerned with meaningless pleasantries and making someone feel good for the sake of feeling good. Jesus was much more concerned about getting to the point that would change some-one's life for the better (so they could experience abundance) and so he dove right into the heart of his mission. We know this related to his mission by keeping our primary scripture in mind from John 10:10 (**"I am come that they might have life"**).

REVIEW THE CLUES

So, what does he tell this highly intelligent, influential, profoundly religious man? "You must be born again." He then detailed what it meant to be born again, which consists of essentially two parts—1) being born of the water and 2) being born of the Spirit.

Just as Nicodemus was confused by the statements Jesus made, so are many today. They assume what it means to be born again, rather than digging in as scripture implores us to do

(**"Study to shew thyself approved unto God, a workman that needeth not to be ashamed, rightly dividing the word of truth."** 2 Timothy 2:15) They think by repenting of their sins and perhaps getting baptized that they have accomplished the feat of being born again, never realizing they are missing the biggest piece of what Jesus said.

Scripture tells us we are to understand the mysteries of God (**"Even the mystery which hath been hid from ages and from generations, but now is made manifest to his saints."** Colossians 1:26) Since a mystery is meant to be solved, there must be some sleuthing involved to solve it or reach a conclusion.

Let's investigate, shall we? When Jesus said we must be born again, the word "again" in Greek is *anōthen* (pronounced an'-o-then) and means "from the beginning or from above."[1] There is our first clue. If the life Jesus came to give us was initially stolen away by a thief (as we can clearly see by the beginning phrase of John 10:10), then we return to the point before it was stolen, back to the beginning, to see when this life began and from where it stems.

Our next clue is the word "beginning," because we recognize the very first book—the beginning—of the Bible is the book of Genesis. This word "Genesis" means beginnings. Therefore, this points us to start our search for life in this book.

When we begin our journey through the first few chapters of Genesis, we learn that God spoke all things into existence: land, trees, seas, fish, whales, birds, animals, sun, moon, stars, seasons—everything. However, one thing we note in Genesis 2:7 when God created man, he didn't speak him into existence like everything else. Rather, it tells us,

"And the Lord God formed man of the dust of the ground, and breathed into his nostrils the breath of life; and man became a living soul."

This is important because it shows us that God got personally, intimately involved with this creation. How do we know it was intimate? By continuing with the verse, we see that God breathed "the breath of life" into man and man became a living soul. We could say that man became alive by the very kiss of God, and a kiss is pretty intimate.

What's even more interesting is that the word "breath" in Hebrew is *nᵉšāmâ* (pronounced nesh-aw-maw') and also means "wind or spirit."[2] Why is this interesting you ask? Because we know according to John 4:24 that ***God is a Spirit.*** If God is a Spirit and he breathed Spirit into man so that man became a living soul, then we must ask ourselves, where did God get the Spirit that he put into man? Obviously, we can only conclude it came from God himself, that it was a part of himself, which he gave to man. Therefore, we could say that God put a part of himself into man, which is why man became alive or had life. (This is also a big clue as to why only Jesus could give us life.)

We presume that man was alive physically after being formed prior to receiving the "breath of life" since scripture makes a distinction that after God breathed into him the thing that came to life was his soul, which means he was now alive spiritually. We conclude man is alive in two ways—first in the flesh (the physical realm) and secondly alive in spirit (the supernatural realm). When the thief stole away this life as we read in Genesis chapter three, it must have been the spiritual life or the supernatural that was taken. We experience physical life in the here and now, but the sense of the supernatural is much harder to find.

AN UNDETECTIBLE SOURCE AND PHYSICAL EVIDENCE

But it was this spiritual life that Jesus shared with Nicodemus in their secret evening discourse. Nicodemus didn't quite understand what Jesus meant by having to be born again so he offered a rhetorical question when he asked, "How can I enter my mother's womb again?" Nicodemus thought physically, but Jesus redirected him to the spiritual realm. Jesus reminded Nicodemus he was a teacher of the spiritual to others (a Pharisee), and now Jesus was simply teaching him more about the spiritual realm.

Notice Jesus indicated there is an undetectable source for the Spirit as he equated it to the wind—you cannot pinpoint the source of wind, but there is evidence of Spirit just as there is evidence of wind when it blows. Likewise, Jesus connected the physical realm with the spiritual realm. In other words, he said that you may not know the spiritual cause but there is a physical manifestation, appearance, or evidence when being born of the Spirit occurs in the physical world.

On a quick side note, we must recognize that Nicodemus doesn't inquire about being born of water. History has clearly shown us that Nicodemus understood the reference to water baptism, because when the Jewish people ushered a new believer (or a proselyte) into the Jewish faith, they baptized them. Archeology has discovered hundreds of small pools called mikvehs for washing sheep throughout the city of Jerusalem that would have been used for this purpose, too. Therefore, Nicodemus understood this reference and was more inquisitive about what he didn't grasp yet and focused on what it meant to be born of the Spirit.

We also see that baptism was widely understood by the Jewish community when we look at the events surrounding John the Baptist. As John was baptizing people, they didn't ask what he was doing (questioning the act), they understood that. Rather they asked why he was doing it (why he was baptizing Jews). He told them he was trying to prepare them for one who would baptize (flood or overwhelm) them in the Spirit.

Now, we can understand that being born again or born of the Spirit means having God's Spirit placed back within us like when God first created man and breathed into him the breath of life. But what is the evidence that this has happened?

Before we can answer that, let's also grab hold of another clue. The word used for "Spirit" in John chapter three is the Greek word *pneuma* (pronounced pnyoo'-mah) and essentially means a movement of wind as in "a current of air" or a "blast of breath"[3] which again points us to the story in Genesis since both references are using basically the same words in different languages to get the point across to us.

TO BE BORN

Evidence of the Spirit entering us is not necessarily the wind, but it has a connection, so let's find out what it is. Since Jesus used the reference of birth, let's look for some clues as to what happens with physical birth and equate them to spiritual birth. Ideally in the physical, there is a desire for each other to be known intimately. We make this same connection spiritually when we realize our need for God and yearn to know him more.

Then there is conception—the seed and the egg combine and start becoming one. There is something similar that happens in the spiritual realm. The *seed* is the word of God. We are clearly told this in the parable of the farmer sowing the seed into the world as found in Luke 8:11, **"Now the parable is this: The seed is the word of God."** The *egg* is our heart or our very being. When we decide to grab hold of the word of God and believe in it and act upon it, we call this faith in the spiritual realm, but it is equivalent to conception in the physical realm. The word has taken hold of our hearts and our hearts have taken hold of the word. Just like the egg can't disregard any genes it does not like before conception; our hearts should not disregard any of God's word before we decide we want to live by it. It's an all or nothing concept, anything else is a deformity waiting to happen.

Next in the physical birth, there is growth and development that takes place in the womb. This occurs in new believers as well. As we read and pray, we discover more about God and what he asks of us, and as we continue in what we know and adjust as we learn, we can develop and grow. If we reject something along the way that God is trying to show us, again we are disrupting our spiritual birth and are putting ourselves at risk.

For a baby to become healthy and reach the point of delivery it must remain attached to the mother via the umbilical cord and the placenta. This connection is one of blood for nourishment and growth. As a believer we must realize Jesus shed his blood to free us from our sin and provide for our growth in him. We must never forget this, and we must continually value the price paid in blood for our souls.

Then comes the baby's delivery. In those moments, the water breaks and the baby passes through it. Baptism is a symbol for us that we are passing through the physical to the spiritual realm. **"Therefore we are buried with him by baptism into death: that like as Christ was raised up from the dead by the glory of the Father, even so we also should walk in newness of life."** (Romans 6:4) The baby then passes through the blood of the one who is bringing it to life. Again, this is a reference to baptism, where the blood of Jesus washes us clean from our sins.

Once a baby is fully in the physical world, the delivery doctor wants to hear signs of new life—the baby crying. This tells the doctor that the baby is taking in air and has breath. To make sound, air enters and exits the lungs creating something like wind. This is like being born of the Spirit and where the reference to the wind connects. Jesus associated the wind with being born of the Spirit. We also see this in the events of the day of Pentecost as described in Acts 2:1–4, **"And when the day of Pentecost was fully come, they were all with one accord in one place. And suddenly there came a sound from heaven as of a *rushing mighty wind*, and it filled all the house where they were sitting. And there appeared unto them cloven tongues like as of fire, and it sat upon each of them. And they were all filled with the Holy Ghost, *and began to speak with other tongues, as the Spirit gave them utterance*."** (Emphasis mine.)

God gave this reference to help us make the connection between what Jesus described to Nicodemus and what the disciples experienced so we would clearly see what is meant to be born of the Spirit. *Hence, everyone who has been filled with God's Spirit will experience this—God speaking through them or what we call speaking in tongues.* Notice that none were left out ("and they were *all* filled") who were gathered together in the upper room seeking God and praying that day. There were 120 of them gathered, not just the apostles—read it for yourself in Acts chapters one and two.

This experience of God refilling his people with his Spirit was given as a promise throughout the Old Testament (see Isaiah 28:11 and Joel 2:28–32 as examples). Even Jesus promised it before he physically left earth (see Mark 16:14–20).

Now the promise was fulfilled (recall what we've learned about promises previously—God will do his part *if* we do our part), as seen in Acts chapter two. The good news is that this promise extends to all humanity throughout the rest of time (see Acts 2:38–39). Therefore, this promise is ours today. If we do our part to seek God and simply ask him to fill us with his Spirit after we have repented, he will then do his part and fulfill his promise by placing his Spirit within us. When we allow God to fill us with his Spirit, once again breathing life into our souls, or resuscitating our spiritual being, then the vacuum caused by sin is properly filled.

CASE CLOSED

This is the mystery revealed or solved as Paul described to the Colossians in chapter 1 verses 26–27, **"even the mystery which hath been hid from ages and from generations, but now is made manifest to his saints: to whom God would make known what is *the riches of the glory of this mystery* among the Gentiles; which is Christ in you, the hope of glory."** (Emphasis mine.)

What are the greatest riches one could ever possess? "Christ in you." How can one know that Christ is in them? It would seem cruel to say that we can have the Spirit within but then be left wondering if we have him or not. Since **"God is not**

the author of confusion" (1 Corinthians 14:33), I don't think he would play that game. To eliminate confusion, he offered evidence that it has indeed occurred. Just like evidence is offered in a court of law, God provided the evidence he said he would when Jesus instructed Nicodemus as proof we have been born again.

Many may not agree, but it does not change the truth of this. Truth is still truth even if others disagree. God does not force his Spirit upon anyone since he has given us all the freedom of choice and force violates that freedom. God is a gentleman and only provides it to those who want it, desire it, and simply ask for it. **"Ask, and it shall be given you; seek, and ye shall find; knock, and it shall be opened unto you: for every one that asketh receiveth; and he that seeketh findeth; and to him that knocketh it shall be opened."** (Matthew 7:7–8)

Some will even argue that they have not experienced speaking in tongues but still believe they have been filled with the Spirit. However, there is no other evidence given in scripture to prove that we have been filled with God's Spirit. Therefore, we must recognize that there is a difference between being influenced by the Spirit and being filled with the Spirit. To be influenced by God, where he shows us truth and guides us closer to him, happens to every believer who honestly desires to know more about God. God will guide us and lead us with his Spirit as he woos us to enter the fullness of truth. However, we can choose along the way how far we will follow him. I like to say we can have as much of God as we want. The more we pursue truth, the more it will be revealed to us. Once we shut truth down with unbelief, that's as far as we can go until we open ourselves back up to truth once more.

FULLNESS OF TRUTH

If our abundance core is to be centered around the proper spirit, then that spirit must embrace truth—the fullness of truth—there is no other way. Imagine a spiritual core that does not embrace the fullness of truth. That means lies or falsehoods can creep in and the center is structured on a cracked foundation, ready to fall apart at any point.

According to John 14:6, **"Jesus saith unto him, 'I am the way, the truth, and the life: no man cometh unto the Father, but by me.'"** If Jesus is the truth, and he said we must be born again, was he lying? If so, he is not the truth—if not, then we must embrace what he said about being born again. We must understand it, embrace it, and follow it. Once we have a solid spiritual core built upon truth, then we can begin to discover meaningful abundance. And like a drop in a pond that radiates with ripples outward, we will begin to see how this spiritual core allows for spiritual abundance in our lives.

Note, if you would like to know more about being born again, obtain a copy of my booklet *"What Does It Mean To Be Born Again."* This brief contemporary and easy-to-comprehend booklet describes the spiritual new birth experience in terms of a physical birth. You can make sure for yourself that you have indeed been born again according to the manner in which God intended. Understanding the words of Jesus will move you into a deeper, more meaningful relationship with God and allow you to experience the new birth in a full, enriching, and rewarding manner. Get your copy at **www.WisdomWell.guru/products**

┌─**TAKE AWAYS**─────────────────────────────┐
· To have an abundant life, we must first have life which
└──┘

begins with birth. Therefore, to have a spiritual core from which proper abundance can flow outward to every other area of our life, we must experience a spiritual birth similar to our physical birth.

- Jesus is not concerned with meaningless pleasantries and making someone feel good for the sake of feeling good. He is more concerned about changing lives for the better, so they can experience abundance. Therefore, his words are meant for impact. They are precise and meaningful—there is no fluff, mixed message, or deceit found in them. His words are truth, but it's up to us if we will receive and act upon them as such. (**"And ye shall know the truth, and the truth shall make you free."** John 8:32)

- We have a responsibility to discover the mysteries of God for ourselves—to dig in and understand the full impact of Jesus's words. While his words are full of truth, they are also layered with meaning. To discover abundance, it will take work to study and understand. Hence, we must take the clues as provided and work to discern the revelation intended for us.

- God is a Spirit and he put part of his Spirit in man. It's at that moment that man became a living soul and had spiritual life. However, the thief in the garden stole this life right out of man, so to be brought back to life we need the infilling of God's Spirit once more.

- Being born of water is to be baptized. Just as there is water with a physical birth that acts as a conduit to usher in a baby from the unknown to the known, there is water involved in our spiritual birth that ushers a believer from the known to the unknown. This association of water is tied closely to the blood of the one giving birth in the physical because as the water comes forth, blood will mingle with it during delivery. Hence in baptism, the blood of the one who provides spiritual birth will be applied to the one being born through the interaction of water.

• Being born of the Spirit is to be filled with God's Spirit and there is evidence that lets us know this has happened, so we don't have to guess. When God places his Spirit within us, he will speak through us a language we didn't learn on our own. We call this experience talking in tongues (or the Pentecostal experience because the first time we see it in Scripture is on the day of Pentecost). There are several descriptions of this happening to believers in scripture to help encourage us (see Acts 2:1–4, Acts chapters 8, 10 and 19), but it is up to us to ask God for it and then earnestly expect to receive it.

• Truth is still truth even if others disagree with it.

NEXT STEPS

If you have not experienced the infilling of God's Spirit within you as evidenced by speaking in tongues, which is an inseparable part of the new birth experience, you can today. Remember all it requires is for us to acknowledge our sin before God (not necessarily before man), to sincerely apologize for our failures coupled with the desire to want to change for the better, voiced in a prayer of our own words, which we call an act of repentance. Then we can ask God to fulfill his promise and fill us with his Spirit. We can be confident that he will do his part.

However, it may take a while to receive this promise, as God knows our hearts better than we do and he will provide it in his timing. If you have been seeking this promise for a while, and still have not experienced it, I would encourage you to talk to another believer who has had this experience—perhaps even a pastor. It may be that there needs to be a further understanding of scripture or of repentance. It may be that you need to understand how to thank and praise God and receive a gift (for that is what the promise is called in scripture—Acts 2:38). Scripture also tells us that God inhabits the praise of his people (Psalm 22:3), so when we ask God for this great gift, we should praise him and thank him for it.

If it's been a while since you've experienced the moving of God in your life and spoken in tongues, ask God for a refilling or a refreshing. At times life gets in the way and we get bogged down with our mistakes, but we can always turn to God and seek his forgiveness and infilling. Simply call out to him today and be amazed once again.

TRANSITION

Now that we understand what it means to have the right spiritual core and how to bring that to life within us, the next thing we must dive into is the understanding of spiritual abundance. Let's jump over to the next chapter and grab hold of this concept.

6
SPIRITUAL ABUNDANCE

*"And ye are complete in him, which is
the head of all principality and power."*
–Colossians 2:10

My heart was pounding unbelievably fast. What was I doing? This wasn't like me. I was taught not to talk to strangers let alone pick them up in my car, but here I was about to do just that. At least it was in broad daylight, which made me feel a little safer but still I was in an area of Milwaukee that I wasn't used to, picking up a stranger with whom I had a brief encounter only days before. Again, this wasn't like me at all, but I knew it was something I had to do.

It all started months earlier. I was praying to be used by God for some greater purpose, because that's what having a proper spiritual core does for you. It makes you hunger for, be a part of, and want to interact with the supernatural.

As a result of those prayers, I felt I was to street preach in downtown Milwaukee. Having never preached anywhere before I wasn't sure what that meant, so I put it off and wrestled with whether it was truly God or not. Then at one Sunday night service I heard a captivating guest evangelist. He talked about winning the lost, then looked directly at me and with authority said, "Are we ready to go out to the streets and reach them?" He looked away and continued his message, but my heart was touched. I knew God was speaking directly to me.

So the next morning, since I was out of work at the time, I went to the church early to pray. I prayed asking what God wanted me to do and began sensing some very specific details—to go to downtown Milwaukee and witness to people on Wisconsin Avenue from 11:00 a.m. to 2:00 p.m. the next day. As I prayed, I followed the "prayer clock" prayer formula (you can find this prayer formula in my book *"God's Promises: A Prayer Journal"*) which usually helped me proceed through my prayer time because it has twelve suggested topics to pray for about five minutes each, and when done I would have prayed for an hour. As a new believer, this was very helpful for me. The areas of the prayer clock were praise, forgiveness, confession, petition, intercession, reading the word, mediating, thanksgiving, praying the word, listening, singing and praise once again.

I had completed everything on the prayer clock except for the singing, and I still didn't know the topic of what I was supposed to witness about the next day in Milwaukee. I was very nervous and very concerned. Since I was the only one in the church at the time and there was sufficient sunlight coming through the windows of the sanctuary, I hadn't turned on the lights. When I decided to leave, I started walking down the center aisle but when I reached the last pew, there was a flash of bright light on my right side, and I was physically pushed over to my left as though I just bumped into something.

Immediately a wave of fear swept over me, but as soon as it did, the thought occurred to me that every time anyone in the Bible encountered angels of the Lord (described as beings of light) they were told not to fear. As soon as that thought finished going through my mind, a wave of peace I had never felt before washed over me, removing the fear. I asked God, "What do you want me to do?" I felt I was to sing, since it was the only thing on the prayer clock I hadn't done yet.

GOD'S INSTRUCTIONS

Instantaneously a chorus to a worship song came to my mind and I began singing it. I sang it over and over a few times, but I couldn't recall the rest of the song. Now to admit my age, this was in the days we used transparent overheads to project the song lyrics onto the wall so the congregation could sing along without holding onto a book or piece of paper. I thought to myself, "I'll find the song in the transparencies," since they were kept in a small crate on the front pew. I went to the crate and located the song, however, between it and the next song was a cassette tape. (Yes, these were also the days we listened to cassettes.) Our church used to record our pastor's messages on cassette and sell them cheaply to anyone who wanted one. This was a strange place for a cassette to be (there were no other cassettes in the crate—I checked), so I read the title and its topic was regarding the second coming of Jesus. I felt I was to listen to it.

I took it home with me, listened to the tape, and afterward felt led to type something. I quickly typed and designed two complete pages of material with each page representing an independent thought or topic that I felt I could use for my street preaching in Milwaukee the next day.

The next morning, I was at the church and made copies of what I had typed (and returned the cassette). I felt directed to make 175 dual-sided copies (one topic on each side of the page) to distribute in Milwaukee. However, because I wasn't' too familiar with the church's copier, I ended up with 175 copies of each topic, meaning I had 350 sheets of paper rather than only the 175 I was supposed to have.

Just as I finished, my pastor entered, and I shared with him what I was doing. I also told him how nervous I was to be doing this alone and he suggested I take another congregant, Brett, who was also out of work at the time. Since I knew him and thought he'd be helpful, I called him, and he agreed to come with me. My pastor also suggested rather than going all the way to downtown Milwaukee, which was about an hour drive, that we just go to the local park in Waukesha, where they were setting up for a festival which was to start the next day.

OBEDIENCE TO GOD REQUIRED
Following my pastor's recommendation, we went to the park and tried talking to several people but because they were busy no one took a flyer or really paid us any attention. Like the grey clouds that were rolling in above us, I began feeling a heaviness roll over me in my spirit that I had never experienced and felt like we still needed to go to Milwaukee. Brett agreed and so we went.

We arrived downtown and parked at the only place I knew to park, since I had only been to a few places in Milwaukee. Having been unemployed for a while, I only had three dollars in my pocket and that's exactly how much it cost to park. We each grabbed a stack of papers and started down Wisconsin Avenue.

I had not looked at the time previously, but as we started walking, I looked at my watch. It was exactly 11:00 a.m. The sun was back out, and people were beginning to flood the street as it was getting close to lunch time. We began talking to people and handing out the flyers I made. Everything was going great, people were friendly, smiling, and taking the pages, but then Brett suggested we move over one street to Michigan Avenue, and I said, "OK."

When we started down Michigan Avenue the clouds blocked the sun once again and no longer were people friendly or accepting what we had to offer. The heaviness came back over me, and I told Brett we needed to go back to Wisconsin Avenue. Thankfully, he agreed. Once we were back on the correct street, the sun appeared again, and people were once more smiling and accepting of us. It was very surreal.

I approached a large black man leaning back against the railing of the bridge and asked him how he was. His response grabbed my attention as much as if he had physically grabbed me. He said in a deep bass voice, "What do you care?" I responded that I really did care and asked him his name. He said Emmanuel. (For those of you who don't know, the name Emmanuel means, "God with us.") I asked, "Emmanuel, how are you?" and he simply said, "I'm hungry!"

I paused what may have been only moments, but it felt like an eternity in my mind, wondering what I could do for him to show that I cared. I just spent my last three dollars; I had no cash and no easy way to get any. I couldn't take him anywhere at that moment because I had a responsibility to Brett. I was perplexed, but then I recalled I had a prepaid phone card in my pocket. (I know I'm really dating myself now, but a prepaid phone card meant you could use a local pay phone for free.) I took it out, gave it to him, and said, "I know you won't believe me, but I have no money right now. If you will take this card and this page, which has my phone number on it and call me tomorrow, I will take you to get something to eat—I promise." He swiped it out of my hand and begrudgingly said, "Yeah," as though he didn't believe me and wanted to just get rid of me.

Brett and I talked to a few more people and suddenly I felt like we were done. Again, I realized I hadn't looked at my watch, so I wondered what time it was and upon glancing at my watch realized it was 2:00 p.m. We counted the pages we had remaining between us, and we had only 175 left, which meant we had delivered 175 pages out of the 350 we started with, just as I had been instructed to in prayer.

After a few days Emmanuel finally called and asked me if I meant what I said about taking him to get something to eat. I said sure and asked where I could find him. He gave me an address, and now I was back in Milwaukee to pick up this stranger.

I was a little frightened when he came to the car as he was quite a big man, I hadn't noticed when he had been leaning on the railing of the bridge, but he was at least six feet six and very broad. I didn't know where to take him for lunch locally, so I drove him back to Waukesha to a buffet where he could eat whatever he wanted and as much as he wanted. I have never seen someone eat so much. The ride gave us time to talk about his situation.

To make this long story at least shorter, I took Emmanuel out to eat several times and learned he was homeless. Over several months through some friends in our church, we found lodging for him, obtained some clothes, landed him a job, and he started attending our church and was filled with the Holy Spirit.

TO PRODUCE SPIRITUAL RESULTS

Why did I include this very lengthy tale here in a chapter entitled spiritual abundance? It's because when we have the right spiritual core, it drives us out of our comfort zone into the realm of the supernatural. I am not someone with special talents or abilities but because I was willing to say yes to the directions of God (and not even perfectly), he was able to move through me to reach Emmanuel and change his life.

Some think spiritual abundance is simply having enough time to pray and read the word of God each day. They feel that by doing so they gain a deeper understanding of God and his working in their lives. While it's good to pray and read the word of God, and I would highly recommend it to everyone, it is still not enough.

Some will bring up Romans 10:17, **"So then faith cometh by hearing, and hearing by the word of God."** This does not mean our faith only comes by hearing the Bible preached to us. It means that we should deeply consider it and implement or carry it out in our daily living—and by doing so, our faith will grow.

Simply reading the Bible and praying helps us get a knowledge of God into our spirits but it doesn't necessarily increase our understanding or help us exercise wisdom. Yes, there are differences between knowledge, understanding, and wisdom. Knowledge is about knowing something or having recall—it's the *what*. It's like going on the game show *Jeopardy* and having the answers to the questions because you know the facts.

Understanding, however is combining your knowledge with the *why*. In other words, its comprehending how the facts fit together, or why they happened. Lastly, wisdom is knowing *what to do* with your knowledge and understanding. It assists in carrying out your actions and knowing what decisions to make.

Scripture motivates us to gain knowledge: **"The heart of the prudent getteth knowledge; and the ear of the wise seeketh knowledge."** (Proverbs 18:15) But we shouldn't stop there because knowledge alone makes us heartless. We should also pursue understanding and by doing so we can help our fellow man through teaching and application. If we want to exercise the supernatural then we absolutely must gain wisdom. These three build upon each other. You cannot have understanding without knowledge, and you can't have wisdom without understanding.

"How much better is it to get wisdom than gold! And to get understanding rather to be chosen than silver!" (Proverbs 16:16) Notice the quality difference of gold versus silver, one increases over the other. Silver represents the repentance of man, which allows man to come into God's presence, just like our understanding allows us to realize our need for God. Gold on the other hand, represents the purity and presence of God, just like wisdom will move us from an understanding that we need God to truly pursuing him in all that we do.

> **He that getteth wisdom loveth his own soul: he that keepeth understanding shall find good.** (Proverbs 19:8)

> **The fear of the Lord is the beginning of wisdom: a good understanding have all they that do his commandments: his praise endureth for ever.** (Psalm 111.10)

How does this apply to spiritual abundance? If we only know about God, we have no practicalities to draw from to help others, and our faith can be shaken in difficult times. If we have some understanding about how God operates, we shore up our faith, but again we don't know how to translate it to others when they ask us about our faith. When we have wisdom, we gain experience from the things we go through, and those experiences create an abundance from which we can reflect the things of God to others.

> **And not only so, but we glory in tribulations also: knowing that tribulation worketh patience; And patience, experience; and experience, hope: and hope maketh not ashamed; because the love of God is shed abroad in our hearts by the Holy Ghost which is given unto us.** (Romans 5:3-5)

Maintaining a proper spiritual core takes vigilance and exercise! It doesn't come easily, and it will cost you everything, but it will be well worth it to experience the supernatural in your life.

> **Then said Jesus unto his disciples, "If any man will come after me, let him deny himself, and take up his cross, and follow me."** (Matthew 16:24)

> **Verily, verily, I say unto you, He that believeth on me, the works that I do shall he do also; and greater works than these shall he do; because I go unto my Father.** (John 14:12)

Why does Jesus make this statement? Perhaps it's because God is supernatural rather than natural. He exists fully in the spiritual realm and is revealed in the natural (physical) realm. On the other hand, we humans exist (at least on the surface) in the natural realm and God is revealed to us in the spiritual realm. Once we establish a proper spiritual core, we begin to understand that we truly exist in the spiritual realm and reveal it in the present. The only way we reveal it in the present is by allowing God to move through us in acts we call supernatural. We could say that it is natural for God to be supernatural—and if he's going to work through us those works would also be supernatural.

FOR GREATER WORKS

Now let's answer the question, how can we do works that are greater than those Jesus did? The answer truly is that we can't! Not in and of ourselves. However, when God places his Spirit within us as described in the previous chapter, we are open to allowing him to flow through us in any way or means he desires. This is how he operated in Jesus. Jesus was the fleshly body for the Spirit of God to flow into the natural world. We, too, become a fleshly tool for God's Spirit to flow through us to others to meet their needs.

Let's combine the understanding that we are a pipeline through which God flows with the concept of spiritual abundance. We recall that abundance in its simplest terms means we have more than enough to share with others. Once we have God within us, we have everything we ever need. We are complete in him! We've been born again and have a promise of eternity. We may feel we still have needs that God hasn't met like physical healing or financial relief. However, when God said we must be born again, he didn't say we needed to be in perfect physical or financial health to be born again. We simply needed to get into right relationship with him. Therefore, when God fills us with his Spirit and we've experienced the evidence that confirms it, we can rest assured that we have everything we need spiritually. Therefore, anything more by definition is abundance.

Now don't misunderstand me. I'm not saying our relationship with God will stop experiencing growth and development the moment we are born again. It's realistic to expect that it will and should continue to grow and expand. I'm saying if God chose to take us out of the physical realm to be in the spiritual realm permanently, then we would have everything we needed (God within us) to exist fully in that realm. Yet, God chooses to leave most of those he fills with his Spirit here in the physical realm to affect others. As our relationship grows and expands it's like increasing the size of the pipeline through which God can flow and therefore affect and influence others either in volume or impact.

There are, however, wrong spirits that can creep in and affect us even after we've been filled with God's Spirit. Pride can clog the pipeline when we start believing we are somehow better than anyone else simply because God is using us in the supernatural to help others. We might be tainted with the thought that there is something special about us that is lacking in others—again, pride—and this is disgusting to God. Pride acts like sludge in the pipeline and after a while will block the flow. There are other things too that drag us from the spiritual back to the physical realm and make us ineffective for God, especially if we start associating finances with how God uses us. If we are Christian artists (musician, actors, speakers, etc.) or in ministry of some kind and we earn a living from our spiritual life, we might only move in the supernatural when we get paid, rather than when God prompts. This is dangerous ground, and we need to regularly keep ourselves in check.

ONLY ONE THING IS NECESSARY

The only thing required by God in being used by him for his purposes is a sincere relationship. It's only about you and him—nobody and nothing else! *Period*! Don't ever let anyone tell you otherwise. You must keep yourself in close contact with God and understand what he is asking of you at any moment in time. I can't stress enough that we are human and make mistakes, but God is gracious and offers us a channel of communication to clear things up called repentance. Let's be completely honest with God and talk to him like the dear friend and father he is—tell him like it is and ask for his help.

I can't stand it when someone says they think I'm religious and they are not. To me religion is not relationship—it implies rituals and routines, which is not at all what God asks of us. He wants something more meaningful. Please don't mistake being spiritual for relationship with God either. Being spiritual can mean you are sensitive to the things of God but doesn't necessarily mean you are in a good relationship with him.

The only way you can have spiritual abundance in your life is through a good and right relationship with God. That means you must understand what God likes and doesn't like. He told us what those are in his word—the Bible.

When we are maintaining that right relationship with God (growing and developing in spiritual terms) and when we've been born again spiritually, we have everything we need. Anything God chooses to do in or through us is considered spiritual abundance (greater things). The more we open the pipeline and allow God to operate the more spiritual abundance will flow. It is exciting and even thrilling to know God has chosen to use you to touch another human life so they can get to know him as well. To maintain this abundance let's be sure to routinely humble ourselves and acknowledge and thank God.

TAKE AWAYS

- Obedience to God's instructions is required to see spiritual abundance in our lives. In our obedience to God, we open a pipeline through which God can flow to meet the needs of others, so they too can experience him in their lives.

- Obedience rests upon relationship. If we have the right relationship with God, we will be obedient to what he asks of us.

- Relationship rests upon knowledge, understanding, and wisdom. The more we know about something the better we feel about it. The more we understand the why behind what we know, the more we can comprehend it and move closer to acceptance of it. Lastly, when we utilize the correct application of our understanding and knowledge, the more successful we will be in our decision making. Therefore, to have a proper relationship with God, we must first know him, then begin to understand him, and lastly apply what we know and understand to our daily living.

- When we have God's Spirit within us, we have everything we need spiritually. We are complete in him. Everything else becomes abundance. Hence, when God moves through our lives to bless others and draw them to him, we call this spiritual abundance.

- We must be on the lookout for things that can upset our spiritual abundance. Things that block the flow of God in our lives like pipeline sludge (pride, for example) can get in the way of what God desires to do in and through us. To clear the pipeline, we must periodically revisit repentance and talk to God frankly and honestly about our lives.

- The only requirement God has in place for us to be used by him in the supernatural is for us to maintain a close, personal, and honest relationship with him. Therefore, do whatever is necessary to ensure it; spend time in prayer, read his word, study, and seek understanding.

NEXT STEPS

When we are born again and have the proper spiritual core within our being, a natural desire should arise to be used by God in the supernatural. Whether it be to pray for others, share our testimony, see the sick healed, the dead raised, or even the miraculous occur, something should stir within that says, "Use me, God, however you see fit." This is because we have been made complete in him and as we grow in relationship with God, spiritual abundance will result in wanting others to know him too.

If you feel this desire within you, then spend some time in prayer asking God what you can do for him. Listen for any specifics then do your best to be obedient to carry out those tasks. If you are unsure or hesitant about what you feel God wants you to do, then seek godly counsel and further prayer for clarification. Wait upon God and he will bring the clarity you need as you continue in prayer.

If you are not feeling these desires yet, then spend time with God in his word and in prayer. Seek to know him better. Ask for further understanding of who he is and let that understanding drive you to utilizing wisdom in your life to impact your decisions. As you grow in your knowledge, understanding, and wisdom, trust that your relationship with God will improve and lead you to a place of deeper obedience, which will propel you into a fuller desire to be used by him.

TRANSITION

Since we have a good understanding of our spiritual core and the meaning and purpose of spiritual abundance, we can now begin to let that understanding spill over into the other areas of our lives and learn how and what that means in terms of those areas. It was necessary for us to address the spiritual core, the God component or the G of our mnemonic device M.I.G.H.T. first to lay the proper foundation. Now that we have done that, we can move back to the beginning of our device with M, our mental component. I mentioned in previous chapters that we will use the M to explore both our mental and emotional areas of life, since our emotions spring from our mental capacities. We feel what we think about. However, we will break down our mental and emotional abundance into separate chapters for better understanding. Therefore, up next; mental abundance.

7
MENTAL ABUNDANCE

"Clarity within leads to clarity without."
–DAVID DILLARD-WRIGHT

TURNED AND ASKED my friend "What did she just say to me? I was just talking to her but for the life of me, I can't remember a single thing she said!"

My mind was mush. I literally could not recall what had been said to me just seconds previously. That is what marijuana did to my mind. Unfortunately, before I developed a meaningful relationship with God, I experimented with marijuana a few times. The last time I tried it, it totally wiped out my short-term memory.

I was headed to a cast party with a friend of mine, and he offered me a joint before going into the party. Immediately after smoking it, my heart was racing, and I felt like I was going to die at any moment. What was worse, upon entering the party and talking with people, I had no idea what was said to me or how I responded. That night I clearly did not have mental abundance but just the opposite.

Most of us don't realize that is how we are operating when it comes to the things of God in our lives. We may hear but don't retain, much less implement. If we have not centered ourselves with a proper spiritual core, we might as well be acting like I was at that party. It's only through God that we can have mental clarity or soundness of mind. After all, 2 Timothy 1:7 tells us, **"For God hath not given us the spirit of fear; but of power, and of love, *and of a sound mind*."** (Emphasis mine.)

A SOUND MIND

By contrast, if it's God who gives us a sound mind, then without him what is our mind? To answer that we must understand the Greek for the phrase "of a sound mind," which is *sōphronismos* (pronounced so-fron-is-mos') and means "self-control, and/or moderation."[1]

Knowing this, we can conclude that without God in our thoughts, we tend to be out of control and without restraint. If you simply look around at our society, it won't take long to convince you this is true. It seems most people either do not know how to control themselves or choose to exercise no restraint. The examples of vulgarity on TV, movies, the internet, and social media sites alone should persuade you of that.

You might ask, "Why does it matter?" Without God in our thoughts, anything goes. The only one that matters then is self, so when determining what is proper and good, it's anything that makes one feel good or provides one with what they want. If conflict develops with someone because what I want differs from what they want, then it results in anger, frustration, and sometimes even violence.

We shrink our thinking when all we think about is ourselves. It limits our creativity and insight when we are controlled by self-motivations. As you know by now, our thoughts impact our emotions. You are what you think or as the Bible puts it, **"For as he thinketh in his heart, so is he."** (Proverbs 23:7)

Recall the "th" on the word "thinketh" implies continually. When we dwell on something, that is what we become or feel. If I think long enough about how I was offended, then I'll be feeling angry or resentful in no time. If, however, I think about the one who offended me in terms of their humanity and how I've been like them so many times when I've offended others, I'll soon be feeling forgiveness toward them instead.

EMOTIONAL THINKING

To prove this is true, just study the craft of acting. To teach actors to cry on stage for their roles, they're told to think of something truly sad that happened in their own lives. Simply by thinking about the situation, they find themselves readily able to cry as needed. If it works for actors, it must work for us. When we think too hard or too long about anything, of course we are impacted emotionally by it.

A while back CBS had a television show called *Scorpion*. The main character had a genius IQ but almost no emotional quotient (a measure of a person's level of emotional intelligence—the ability to perceive, control, evaluate, and express emotions). The show was reflective of individuals who spend so much time in higher thought they pay no attention to their emotions and how they affect others. This truly is the result of self-centeredness.

When all one does is think about themselves, what they want, and how they are being affected without any concern about the cares or needs of others, they end up with no emotional quotient. They become delusional when it comes to their own emotions and the emotions of others. Most of us do not relate to or appreciate this quality and will avoid people who are like this. (Perhaps this is why the show was cancelled after only a few seasons.)

This is not what God desires for us. He wants us to have a sound mind. That means he wants us to be able to think clearly and feel clearly. To do so, we must take our thoughts off of self and place them on the needs of others. This was exactly the mind Jesus had as he walked this earth. You can see in every interaction described in scripture that he was focused on the one with whom he was interacting, not on himself. The apostle Paul encouraged us with these words, **"Let this mind be in you, which was also in Christ Jesus."** (Philippians 2:5)

There are other encouragements related to our minds found throughout scripture such as:

Thou wilt keep him *in perfect peace*, whose mind is stayed on thee: because he trusteth in thee. (Isaiah 26:3) (Emphasis mine.)

Jesus said unto him, "Thou shalt love the Lord thy God with all thy heart, and with all thy soul, and with all thy mind." (Matthew 22:37)

And even as they did not like to retain God in their knowledge, God gave them over to a reprobate mind, to do those things which are not convenient. (Romans 1:28)

For they that are after the flesh do mind the things of the flesh; but they that are after the Spirit the things of the Spirit. *For to be carnally minded is death; but to*

be spiritually minded is life and peace. (Romans 8:5–6)
(Emphasis mine.)

And be not conformed to this world: but be ye transformed by the renewing of your mind, that ye may prove what is that good, and acceptable, and perfect, will of God. (Romans 12:2)

But I fear, lest by any means, as the serpent beguiled Eve through his subtilty, so your minds should be corrupted from the simplicity that is in Christ. (2 Corinthians 11:3)

And be renewed in the spirit of your mind; (Ephesians 4:23)

Wherefore gird up the loins of your mind, be sober, and hope to the end for the grace that is to be brought unto you at the revelation of Jesus Christ. (1 Peter 1:13)

So, what do we gather from reading these scriptures? We see again as we focus on ourselves (our flesh or our carnality), that we cannot operate with clarity of mind. In doing so, God will allow us to venture off in our thoughts resulting in a reprobate (perverse, degenerate, depraved) mind. On the other hand, if we trust God and do not conform to what everyone else is doing and thinking, but rather allow him to transform the way we think, we find simplicity, renewal, and sobriety or clarity of mind.

GAINING CLARITY

Once I discovered God wanted me to have a clear head, I decided to completely stop using whatever might cloud my thinking. For example, marijuana, alcohol, or any other drug alters our brain chemistry—even if only momentarily—and hinders our ability to think clearly. The Bible doesn't specifically address marijuana, but it does speak to alcohol. While some will say that scripture doesn't say completely abstain from it, it also doesn't completely condone it either. Take these scriptures for reference:

Do not drink wine nor strong drink, thou, nor thy sons with thee, when ye go into the tabernacle of the congregation, lest ye die: it shall be a statute for ever throughout your generations. (Leviticus 10:9)

Wine is a mocker, strong drink is raging: and whosoever is deceived thereby is not wise. (Proverbs 20:1)

It is not for kings, O Lemuel, it is not for kings to drink wine; nor for princes strong drink (Proverbs 31:4)

But on the other hand, there are these scriptures as well:

Give strong drink unto him that is ready to perish, and wine unto those that be of heavy hearts. (Proverbs 31:6)

Drink no longer water, but use a little wine for thy stomach's sake and thine often infirmities. (1 Timothy 5:23)

Now, I believe the reason for what seems to be conflicting scriptures is that we really are being encouraged to seek moderation. We are not to give ourselves over to these things and lose control or perhaps even hinder our ability to make decisions, which relies upon us having clarity of mind.

(For informational purposes only; please note the Hebrew word for "strong drink" in the scriptures above is šēḵār (pronounced

shay-kawr') and means fermented or intoxicating liquor.[2] And the Greek word for "wine" is oinos *(pronounced oy'-nos) meaning wine literally or figuratively, as from a winepress[3], which leaves it open for interpreting it as grape juice. Now with this information you can decide for yourself.)*

Alcohol (as well as marijuana and other drugs) taints our thinking, so for me it was an easy decision based upon my previous experiences before knowing God to choose to abstain from now on. Medications can affect our brains too, so does that mean I don't take pain medication? Not if I don't have to. If the pain is so bad that I can't think straight, then I will take something. Remember, it's about maintaining your clarity of mind. It might be worth it to understand that even basic foods can have a significant impact on our minds when we consume too much sugar, fat, caffeine, or other chemicals in our food. Perhaps that's why God also prompts us to eat a healthy diet.

This is important, because to have mental abundance one must have clarity of mind. Recall, abundance means having more than enough to share with others. If we are too self-absorbed in thought, we have nothing to spare, give, or bless others with. If we focus on God and obtain clarity of thought, we start to have an excess of thoughts to share with others for their benefit and not our own, which leads to creativity.

How do we know that is the case? Because God is a God of creativity. We see it manifested in the very first book of the Bible when God speaks everything into existence. God creates all kinds of plants, trees, fish, birds, and animals—all unique and different. Then he creates man different from all previous creation. He is a God who expresses himself in creativity. In fact, he is so creative that scientists have studied snowflake crystallization and found that there are no two snowflakes alike. Think about the billions of snowflakes that fall every winter season! That's how creative God is. He cares about the tiniest details, like snowflakes, to make them all different. He made no two humans alike either. Sure, we see twins who on the outside may look the same but upon examination have different thoughts, feelings, expressions, and experiences.

Since scripture informs us that we are made in God's image, if he is creative then it only makes sense that we too should operate in a wide array of creativity. Mental abundance comes through the creativity we can express on behalf of our Creator—and not just in simple creativity. Often our minds think of creativity like, *They must be able to paint well, or sing and write songs, or put down inspiring words in a book.* No, creativity as God describes is in even the small things—how we think through our daily work and problem solve, how we address a need someone may have, or simply an out of the box type of idea to deal with a difficulty we must handle.

Some will point to examples of people who are very creative but may not know God. For example, Elon Musk is described as an atheist or agnostic at best, yet he is a part of several very creative ventures like Tesla Motors and SpaceX. These enterprises have come up with numerous creative ideas, so what if he doesn't acknowledge God in his creativity? How come he has this creative abundance? We must recall that true abundance is established through balance in every area of our lives. God will allow those who don't know him to prosper in certain areas of their lives for the benefit of mankind. This doesn't mean they have abundance in all other areas of their lives. Our focus in this book is discovering abundance in every area of life and the only way to do that is through a proper spiritual core that radiates outward through each area. Hence, the spiritual core we develop must be evident and relevant in our thoughts and emotions.

MASTERING OUR THOUGHTS

Can our thoughts be mastered? Can we bring the wayward thoughts and feelings we have into subjection as the Bible encourages us to do?

> **Casting down imaginations, and every high thing that exalteth itself against the knowledge of God, and *bringing into captivity every thought to the obedience of Christ*.** (2 Corinthians 10:5) (Emphasis mine.)

I believe we can, and this verse is not only the encouragement to do so but is also the key in how to do it. If our minds get caught up with self and our own imaginations, then we must be proactive and submit those thoughts to God for God to prevail. Scripture tells us our thoughts pale in comparison to God's thoughts—wouldn't you want to have the best thoughts possible?

> **For my thoughts are not your thoughts, neither are your ways my ways, saith the Lord. For as the heavens are higher than the earth, so are my ways higher than your ways, and my thoughts than your thoughts.** (Isaiah 55:8–9)

So how do we cast down these negative, useless, or even harmful thoughts? First, we must recognize when they occur, and then we must reject and drive them out. For example, if an unwanted visitor came to your house and rang the doorbell, you probably would go to the door to see who was there. Upon recognizing the visitor, you may or may not let them in, right?

You may be so comfortable with your thoughts that you gave them a key, so they freely let themselves enter. Or perhaps you stopped locking or even closing the door, so they have free access. If you grow tired of their presence in your living space, you may ask them to leave, but they've become so comfortable they don't want to go. If you truly want them gone, you must take greater action and escort them to the door. If you want them to stay gone then you must get radical, reclaim the key, and start locking the door.

Your thoughts won't understand your new behavior. This is strange to them—after all you welcomed them so many times previously. They will resist because your mind was their home, and they don't want to leave. They will show up at unexpected times, pounding on the door, and their frequency will be annoying and inappropriate. But if you even crack open the door just once, they'll move in again. You must stand your ground to get rid of them. If you stand firm, eventually your thoughts will start bothering you less and less. Occasionally they will still show up out of the blue and try to test the limits, so be alert and consistent.

How do I know this? Because I've been through this. Prior to having a meaningful relationship with Jesus, I was very carnally minded and thought about inappropriate things constantly. I entertained my daydreams and envisioned how I could bring them to life. These thoughts flooded my mind when I was showering, driving to work, trying to work, driving home, anytime, and anywhere. I started thinking I couldn't control them no matter how hard I tried. I knew I wanted to change, but I couldn't.

Until I realized these thoughts were not of God and that God didn't want me entertaining them, I was powerless over them. Once I acknowledged these thoughts didn't come from God, I had to determine where or from whom they came. If I was the one desiring change, they weren't coming from me. That meant the only remaining source was the enemy—the devil. And, if that was true, how was I to handle them? I asked myself, *How did Jesus address the devil and his unwanted thoughts?* I remembered when Jesus was tempted by the devil and also when Peter tried to talk him out of his life's purpose that Jesus rebuked the devil and put him in his place (see Matthew chapter 4 and Mark chapter 8). Since I have no power in and of myself, I need to rely upon the source of all power—Jesus.

And Jesus came and spake unto them, saying, "All power is given unto me in heaven and in earth." (Matthew 28:18)

Neither is there salvation in any other: for there is none other name under heaven given among men, whereby we must be saved. (Acts 4:12)

BEGIN EXPERIENCING REJECTION

When those unwanted imaginations began entering my mind, I said to myself, "Those thoughts are unwanted here, and I rebuke them in Jesus's name!" I surrendered those thoughts to God time and time again, and gradually they subsided and left. I obtained the victory over those nasty thoughts. As I said, they occasionally try to test the limits and I still must rebuke them to conquer them, but they have been put in their place!

Now I experience greater abundance with clearer thoughts and spend time thinking about the needs of others. My emotions have also evened out—I don't constantly ride the waves of intense emotion any longer.

Are there other practical ways we can create mental abundance? There are, but I don't believe they are as important as what we have just described. According to the world, we should take up new hobbies to expand our minds and think in new ways. If we take classes, read books, and have deep discussions, the world's belief is that we will create mental abundance or be able to expand the way we think. While I'm not against these things and believe they do help in some way, I feel they only scratch the surface of what mental abundance really means.

It's true that we should be continually learning and growing. I even pursue CANI (which stands for constant and never-ending improvement), as I learned it from Tony Robbins. This means that in everything we do and think we should be striving to improve in some slight way. Today this is called the pursuit of 1 percent, because behavior theorists stress if you strive to improve in small incremental ways, say 1 percent each day, this will lead to huge gains over the long haul. This is great for mental growth and capacity, but it doesn't necessarily lead to true mental abundance.

One way to help boost the odds of gaining mental abundance is sharing what you've learned or gained with others. We have a responsibility to not let our wisdom die with us but to instill it in those we leave behind. That shifts the way your brain thinks about things and helps you better absorb or retain what you learn. It also helps you focus on helping others, thereby removing yourself from the equation. (We'll talk more about this in a later chapter.) These are only a part of true mental abundance as long as they don't leave out the best part—God. When God is left out, there is no way to obtain the desired abundance because real abundance is a spiritual concept only supplied by him. (You will appreciate this concept even more after reading the next chapter.)

Blessed be the God and Father of our Lord Jesus Christ, who hath blessed us with *all spiritual blessings* in heavenly places in Christ. (Ephesians 1:3) (Emphasis mine.)

Another avenue others promote for mental abundance is meditation. Find quiet time to still your mind, clear it of any thoughts, and just meditate to discover new thoughts and ideas as they come to you. This concept is found throughout many religions and has a strong spiritual connotation to it. In the Christian realm, we might call this prayer—communication with God (I say might because there is a distinction that can be made between prayer and meditation, and you can discover the difference in my book "*God's Promises: A Prayer Journal*"). Communicating with God on a regular basis lets him inspire you with creativity. In essence, meditation or prayer should spring forth from the right spiritual core to receive reliable, pure, and untainted thoughts and ideas—or in other words, inspired creativity.

TAKE AWAYS

- It's only through God that we can obtain a sound mind or possess what we call mental clarity. Without God in our thoughts, we lack self-control and restraint.

- When we are caught up in selfish thinking, we become insensitive to the needs of others. This clouds our thinking and prevents mental clarity.

- Mental clarity is very important to God. He desires that we maintain it so his creativity can flow through us. It's so important to him that he has advised us to avoid things that can impair our thinking, which may include alcohol, drugs, or even certain foods. We must discover a proper balance of what we ingest for our bodies and minds to operate at their optimum.

- God's creativity in us is not limited to what we commonly think of as creative endeavors such as dancing, singing, painting, or writing, but rather is found in the small things like daily problem solving, addressing another's need, or resolving a difficulty.

- We can control negative, harmful, even habitual thoughts by first recognizing them and rejecting them. Second, we subject them to the authority of Christ. We need to do this every time they come at us until eventually we gain the victory. Even after we've triumphed, we must remain diligent to maintain the upper hand.

- There may be other ways to expand our mind and enhance its potential, like eating right, getting enough sleep, learning new things, and meditating. However, there is nothing that is singularly more important to mental abundance than maintaining the right spiritual core. This is because of the significant connection the mind has with the Spirit (see the next chapter) and because mental abundance is really a spiritual concept that only flows out from our connection with God.

NEXT STEPS

I simply ask you take some time to reflect on the common types of thoughts that flow through your mind. Are there certain things you find yourself letting your mind entertain? Are these things helping or hindering your closeness with God? If you desire to be free of negative things or you crave soundness of mind that only God can provide, start taking charge of these thoughts today. When these thoughts come to you, recognize them, reject them, and then submit them to God. For example, the next time you think you are not worthy of love or acceptance, say to yourself, "I reject that lie of the enemy and I give it to God, Now God, help me think about myself the way you think about me." Try to do this as consistently as you can and I'm sure that over time you will notice your thoughts have improved.

TRANSITION

As we gain control over our thoughts and begin to reap the benefits of mental abundance, we will begin to see the ramifications to our emotions. This is because our emotions are tied to our thoughts. Therefore, let's dive into that connection in the next chapter and as we do, we will also begin to see how our thoughts are the connection between the physical realm and the spiritual realm.

8
EMOTIONAL ABUNDANCE

"Emotional intelligence is your ability to recognize and understand emotions in yourself and others, and your ability to use this awareness to manage your behavior and relationships."
–Travis Bradberry

"WHY ARE YOU CRYING?" my wife asked me.

"I don't know, I just feel sad."

Nothing had changed per se—I mean nothing that I didn't expect. I knew for several weeks my son was heading back to school. I wanted him to go back and experience the fullness of his life and the fantastic opportunities college would afford him. Still, after moving him into his new apartment, I was back home and feeling sad. I felt the same way a few years earlier when we moved my daughter into her dorm. I cried then as well, so you'd think I would have been able to handle it better.

That is the power of our emotions. We feel things and they come out—sometimes whether we want them to or not. Have you ever had a thought that made you laugh out loud? Sometimes it seems we can't control our emotions, yet as I pointed out in the previous chapter, our emotions are so closely linked to our thoughts that it's hard to separate them.

Still, there is something that differentiates our emotions. They are strongly connected to our mental capacity. What about the times you've walked into a room and suddenly felt something? Perhaps you attended a wedding reception and the moment you walked in, you felt the love and warmth of the moment flood you with joy. Maybe there were other times you walked into a room where moments before a couple had a tremendous fight and you felt like you could cut the tension with a knife.

A LINGERING FEELING

Emotions linger. They are the expression of the mental release we experience, and they can overwhelm us. Of course, we can control our emotions like we can control our thoughts, as I described previously. However, what about those lingering sensations I'm talking about now?

When emotions are generated by our own thoughts, the connection is direct and able to be managed much better. I realized this even before my relationship with God was solid. When I began taking control over how I felt as a young man, I found a quote I read often and began practicing it frequently. It was this, "Motion changes emotion." I can't tell you where I found this little gem, but I can tell you that I have found it to be priceless. Whenever my emotions are too much for me or I know I need to change them, I get up and do something else—go for a walk, take care of my chores, play a song, or anything that shifts my mind to something else. This breaks the immediate connection of my thoughts with my emotions. My new thoughts will create connections to new emotions. It's that simple and that's part of the premise we already discussed. So, what about when emotions overcome you or hit you out of the blue that you were not initially thinking or feeling? What is that all about? How come you can be affected by someone else's emotions?

Think about how quickly you can be swept up in the emotion of someone who is highly emotional. That's the goal of great orators. They give a moving speech hoping to rouse something within you that gets you moving in the same direction as them. Your own thoughts let you connect with them, but there is an additional element that pulls you along the way.

Recall that I said emotions linger. The part that lingers is what I call the spirit of our thoughts. Some label it as energy, and as Einstein pointed out—energy cannot be created or destroyed, it can only be changed from one form to another. If that's true, then some of the daily calories we consume transform to generate our thinking, which in turn releases our emotions. Therefore, we could call emotions a form of energy. When you walk into a room and feel tension exists it's because somehow that spirit has been released in that room and it is slamming up against you and your spirit. We will discuss why this matters in a minute. For now, let's refer to emotions as the tint of the paint, if you will.

When you go to the store to buy paint, it all starts off as the same base color—a kind of plain milky white. After staring at dozens upon dozens of color swatches to select the right shade for your living room walls, you take the swatch to the salesclerk who keys certain numbers into a machine that injects the milky white paint with various combinations of red, yellow, and blue. Then they stir it all together to create the color you selected. Once mixed, however, there ain't no going back when it comes to paint.

The same goes for emotions. When emotion has been released, it creates a "color" or releases a spirit (energy). How can I prove this?

Let's take alcohol as an example. What is another name for alcohol? Spirits. Why is that? Where did that term originate from? In its basic function, what does alcohol do to someone? It affects their mind. Drink enough of it and you can't think straight. Since it affects the mind, it also affects the emotions. You may hear someone say they drink to get rid of their inhibitions or fears. They might be nervous, so they drink to steady themselves. Said another way they are experiencing the emotions of fear or nervousness and they want to experience the emotion of peace, so they are dulling the mind's thoughts to block the emotion of fear. They hope to experience peace, but of course we know it doesn't work that way. To experience peace, you must have peaceful thoughts.

When someone drinks and becomes drunk, you can easily see they are no longer acting like themselves. In fact, they begin to act like someone or even something else. They do things they wouldn't normally do or say things they normally wouldn't say. This also happens to someone possessed by a spirit and hence the association of alcohol with the word spirits. Generically the term is used because often those who are drunk become giddy or silly, so those who profit from the sale of alcohol began using the word spirits to associate it with an uplifting mood—which is anything but true since alcohol is actually a depressant.

SPIRIT AND LIFE

Let's pause a moment and understand this from a biblical perspective. When Jesus taught his disciples about how they needed to absorb God and digest his truth, he made the statement, **"It is the spirit that quickeneth; the flesh profiteth nothing:** *the words* **that I speak unto you, they** *are spirit,* **and they are life."** (John 6:63) (Emphasis mine.)

Notice he equated his words to spirit. Where do words come from? They come from the thoughts that are then expressed in words. These thoughts and words create emotion (energy) and hence allow for the lingering of spirit (energy). Here are additional scriptures to consider:

For to be *carnally minded* is death; but to be *spiritually minded* is life and peace. (Romans 8:6) (Emphasis mine.)

And be renewed in *the spirit of your mind*. (Ephesians 4:23) (Emphasis mine.)

Only let your conversation be as it becometh the gospel of Christ: that whether I come and see you, or else be absent, I may hear of your affairs, that ye stand fast *in one spirit, with one mind* striving together for the faith of the gospel. (Philippians 1:27) (Emphasis mine.)

Now we beseech you, brethren, by the coming of our Lord Jesus Christ, and by our gathering together unto him, that ye be *not soon shaken in mind, or be troubled, neither by spirit, nor by word,* nor by letter as from us, as that the day of Christ is at hand. (2 Thessalonians 2:1–2) (Emphasis mine.)

These scriptures show us there is a connection between the mind and the spirit. Since emotions come from the expression of our thoughts, which generate from within our minds, they open the door of the spiritual realm. When these emotions are strongly expressed, they leave the lingering of the spirit from which they arose. You could also say spirit reflects attitude. Therefore, if you encounter a spirit of anger, it is because someone had an angry attitude or if someone feels a spirit of jealousy, it's because there is an attitude of jealousy.

THE SPIRIT IMPACT

Are you seeing that the mind is the gateway for the spiritual? It is the connection through which the physical and the spiritual meet. Many refer to spiritual things as energy or auras (an energy glow). While they may be partially correct, they fail to see the whole picture. God is pure energy and God exists in and through everything. Because God existed before anything else, through his existence he then created everything. Therefore, everything exists within him. If God exists within everything that was created in the physical world, then he would have also made a way for the spiritual world to be connected to it, since the essence of God is spiritual.

John said it this way in the opening of his gospel, **"In the beginning was the Word, and the Word was with God, and the Word was God."** (John 1:1) Where do words come from? Thoughts. And the resulting words create emotion or energy. So, we could say that God is energy—in fact, he is the purest absolute form of energy there is, and he gave his energy to all living things that he created. We can see God used the human mind as the connecting point between the physical and the spiritual—specifically our thoughts and resulting words to display this energy—which can be experienced or felt through our emotions. So please don't tell me God is not an emotional God.

There can be no other doorway for the spiritual. The other areas of life, our physical health, for example, cannot be a doorway to the spiritual because we are literally using the term physical here. Our physical health is rooted purely in the physical realm.

Don't misunderstand me here, our physical health can be impacted by spiritual things, but it is not a directly connected doorway linked to the Spirit—it only experiences the effect of the Spirit. That's why when we die in the physical our bodies remain and turn to dust, but our consciousness (our minds) live on. The same goes for our financial lives, as the financial is rooted in the physical realm. Our interactions, that is our social and relational lives, occur here in the physical world as well, even though they are impacted by the spiritual. The results of our interactions are carried out in the physical. All these other areas, of course, have a correlating impact on our emotions because they affect how or what we think about, thereby completing the circle.

I understand this can be a hard concept to grasp, so think of it this way. If a person truly is made up of two aspects—physical and spiritual—then there must be a place these two things meet and touch, allowing a cross over from one to the other. It may be hard or even impossible to see within the physical realm because it's like looking at the skyline across the horizon. As you look at the horizon, you can observe the separation between land and sky, but upon approaching it, the distinction isn't so easy to make out because it shifts further out. It's similar with mind and spirit.

One last thought to demonstrate this—when they crucified Jesus where did they carry out this hideous and grotesque action? **"And he bearing his cross went forth into a place called *the place of a skull*, which is called in the Hebrew Golgotha."** (John 19:17) (Emphasis mine.)

What is the implication here in this scripture? Why does God point this out in his word? Because it is important for us—it's a clue. The place of the skull is where the brain or the mind resides. And the spiritual act of redemption, that is the sacrifice for our sins, took place in this physical location. That means the greatest spiritual battle occurs and can only be won in the physical mind of the believer. Why? Because this is the connection point between the physical and the spiritual.

RESULTING EMOTIONAL ABUNDANCE

Why is any of this important? It is said that human beings only use approximately 10 percent of our brains. But if you connect what I've been describing, it implies we can have mental and resulting emotional abundance with God. I believe God allows the opening of our understanding (our minds) and grants greater use of our minds or what we call abundance. Here are just two verses from Psalm 119 that demonstrate abundance in understanding. **"Through thy precepts I get understanding: therefore I hate every false way."** (Psalm 119:104) **"The entrance of thy words giveth light; it giveth understanding unto the simple."** (Psalm 119:130)

Emotional abundance comes from not being impacted, swayed, controlled, or manipulated by the emotions or spirits of others. Being affected by other spirits or the attitudes of others when it is not in our best interest, deters us from everything we can be. Remember evil spirits are only here to ***"steal, and to kill, and to destroy"*** according to our primary scripture of John 10:10.

To have emotional abundance we must have what the Bible calls *discernment.* That is "the quality of being able to grasp and comprehend what is obscure—not clear or plain."[1] When we walk into a room and feel something is off, we must use discernment, so we aren't caught up in the spirit of lingering emotions driving our thoughts instead of our thoughts driving our emotions. As described in the last chapter, it's similar to subjecting our thoughts to God. We must also submit our emotions to God to help understand the spiritual implications.

Beloved, believe not every spirit, but try the spirits whether they are of God. (1 John 4:1)

When we do so, we experience freedom of emotion and resulting abundance to share with others. Instead of being impacted by the spirit of others, we can impact others with the Spirit of God emanating from us. This is true emotional abundance—having our emotions in check and yet being able to relate to the emotions of others enough to help them gain perspective as well.

Emotional abundance is a result of not allowing our emotions to rule us. It's interesting how few scriptures deal with the word feelings. In fact, if you type in the word "feel" in the online Bible tool at Biblegateway.com it will generate a list of scriptures that contain the word or derivatives of the word "feel" (like feels, or feelings), and only nine appear within the King James version of the Bible. Of those nine scripture references, three deal with physical touch, and only six relate to emotions. On the other hand, the word "spirit" has over 500 scripture references that appear. To me this reveals that our view of God is not to be based upon our feelings. It doesn't mean God does not have feelings. In fact, Hebrews 4:15 says, **"For we have not an high priest which cannot be touched with the feeling of our infirmities; but was in all points tempted like as we are, yet without sin."**

This means Jesus felt the same things we feel, but he didn't let his emotions drive him. He drove his emotions and took them to the cross for our sins so we could experience an abundant life. Remember we are made in God's image. Yes, he is an emotional God, since he feels sorrow, joy, pain, grief, and excitement. Therefore, we must keep in perspective what is truly important—clarity to know God and his will by maintaining a proper relationship with him that isn't driven by emotion only but is driven by pure, controlled, or designated thought.

Realize this as well that God is the source of all intelligent thought according to John 1:1. The use of "word" here in the Greek is *logos* (pronounced log'-os) and means "something said including the thought, reasoning, the mental faculty or divine expression."[2] We get our word logic from this Greek word. Now we can see the connection between the mind and the Spirit, as well as recognize that logic is not based on feeling but on clarity of thought. Perhaps this is why Ecclesiastes 8:5 says, **"Whoso keepeth the commandment *shall feel no evil thing*: and a wise man's heart discerneth both time and judgment."** (Emphasis mine.)

What are some other things we can do to assist with emotional abundance? One thing we must realize is that other people's problems don't have to be our own. I used to think I was responsible for other people's feelings, so I would begin experiencing what they were feeling, which did me no good. To stop this practice in myself I realized that if someone physically threw up all over me, I wouldn't just continue to wear my outfit with the appearance and smell of vomit all over it. I would immediately shower and change clothes, then wash that outfit to remove the traces of vomit from it. It's the same when someone comes to us with their problems. If they emotionally throw up all over us, we don't have to own it. We can sympathize and console where and when needed, but we can also recognize that we are responsible for our own emotional health. We may be impacted by the issue they share with us, but we can find ways to cope and reset ourselves, whether that's through prayer, performing some other activity, or simply choosing to think about something else.

Next, we can watch the words we say about ourselves. It may be OK to be a little self-deprecating at times, but self-destruction is never OK. If the emotions we generate from our thoughts can affect others, then the same is true of the thoughts we think about ourselves. This is why even those who may not acknowledge God will advocate for the use of affirmations. They understand this connection (created and designed by God) and how it works. However, without the interjection of God into this method, it's of limited affect. When combined with the way God sees us and loves us, it can have a tremendous impact resulting in true emotional abundance.

If we want to control our emotions, we must learn to control our tongue and our thoughts. Since there is a strong connection from the thoughts we think to the words we say resulting in the emotions we feel, it is imperative we begin addressing the issue at the source—our thoughts. If we control our thoughts, there is hope we can also control our tongue and have better control over our emotions. You can refer to the previous chapter on how to gain control over your thoughts.

There may be other ideas from a clinical or therapeutic per-spective that can give one an edge and improve emotional abundance. While they may be beneficial and worth looking into, I don't believe they are as helpful as those described here. By incorporating God into our thoughts and emotions, it's a guaranteed win. All other helpful tactics or recommendations should only be applied in relationship to their assistance in maintaining God in the equation.

TAKE AWAYS

- Our emotions are powerful and can appear to have a life of their own. However, every emotion is linked to our thoughts, so any power our emotions receive is granted by our thoughts. If we want to change our emotions, we must change our thoughts.

- Emotions are the result of energy released and as an outcome can linger. We can be unexpectedly impacted by the emotions of others. Therefore, it is important to utilize discernment when we encounter these situations. Allowing God to direct us helps us to not be influenced by these lingering emotions.

- The mind is the gateway for the spiritual. It's the connection God established between the physical and the spiritual. Hence, the greatest spiritual battle occurs within our minds and it's also where we can find victory and experience redemption.

- Emotional abundance is experienced by having control over our emotions and not being negatively impacted by the emotions of others but still being able to relate to others to help them gain perspective.

- To keep from sinking the ship of our emotions we must control the cannons of our lips. Watching what we let loose with our tongue is a huge step toward taking control over our emotional abundance. See the previous chapter to take control over your thoughts and emotions.

NEXT STEPS

How do you generally feel? Are there emotions in you that seem out of control? Are you easily impacted by the emotions of those around you? Sit quietly and think about how you would like your emotions to improve. Ask God to help you with your thoughts around these emotions. Remember we feel what we think. Look back at the previous chapter, if necessary, and start taking control over your thoughts. Submit them and your feelings to God. Trust that God can use the doorway of your physical mind to impart understanding of his Spirit. Allow his word to bring you the energy needed for change and believe he will expand your ability for clear thought and provide emotional abundance in the process.

TRANSITION

I trust you've been learning how the right spiritual core impacts and influences our thoughts and emotions, and you can now see the benefits clearly. The abundance that can be experienced is both exciting and rewarding individually. However, there's more to you than your individuality. You need to interact with others. There's no escaping it. Demands are placed on you from close personal relationships and social connections. In the next couple of chapters let's dig into what abundance looks like relationally and then socially. Remember true abundance must come from having all aspects of our lives functioning well, so we can't neglect these areas.

9
RELATIONAL ABUNDANCE

*"When you stop expecting people to be perfect,
you can like them for who they are."*
–Donald Miller

"SHE REALLY LOVES ME. I believe she really loves me!"

These thoughts were running through my head as my wife and I walked around the neighborhood. We were still considered newlyweds, married for approximately three years. I can't recall the specifics of this moment, even though I recall a lot of the other details. We were still living in our first apartment in Waukesha, Wisconsin. It was a warm summer day. We went on a walk, and I remember my wife wore a long kelly green skirt and a flowered short sleeve top. I was in dress pants and a long sleeve shirt because I just came home from work. I even had on a tie because back then we dressed up for work—business casual wasn't a thing yet.

I recall as we walked, I held her hand and felt so content. It was the greatest feeling I think I ever had, at least up to that point in my life. We didn't talk about earth shattering things. In fact, I can't even remember what we talked about. I would guess we were describing our day and or our plans for the week or weekend ahead. What I vividly recall are the thoughts flooding over me that she loved me, and I *knew* she loved me.

Me of all people. Why me? I'm not sure, but nonetheless it was me she loved.

That's what relational abundance is like. When you are so secure in your relationship and the feelings of love are so strong that you can give more of yourself away, you are surly experiencing abundance. Don't get me wrong here, I didn't have it yet—she did.

A FOUNDATION OF LOVE

My wife made me feel more loved in that moment than I had been my entire life. That was not an easy thing for me to feel, having been through so much rejection, heartache, and pain in my life. Yet she broke through all that past garbage to let me know I was loved.

It didn't happen overnight, and it wasn't some grand gesture she did that made me feel it—it was the several years we spent together through small moments like these that allowed me to believe and accept the love she offered me. She was and still is the kind of person who clearly operates from a place of relational abundance.

> **Greater love hath no man than this, that a man lay down his life for his friends.** (John 15:13)

Please note this scripture does not say greater love is connected to those whom we love the most, or even those who love us back. It says greater love is connected to those we consider friends. The term friend used in this scripture is very loose when it comes to defining a friend. The Greek word is *philos* (pronounced fee'-los) and while it can be interpreted as friends, it also means "to be friendly to one, wish him well, an associate, a companion or a neighbor."[1]

Have you ever considered someone your friend and then been betrayed by that person? I'm sure we've all been in that boat and once discovered, it may have felt like our heart sank. Yes, it's even those people to whom this scripture refers. Jesus demonstrated this for us—when he went to the cross, he hung there dying for all, even those like Judas whom he called friend but who had betrayed him.

This great act of Jesus's demonstrates abundance in human interactions. If you recall, I stated that the letter I in the mnemonic M.I.G.H.T. stands for interactions. But I combined our relational and social lives into this one-word *interaction*, because technically it encompasses both as overall human relations. However, here is where I want to draw some distinction once again between our relational lives and our social lives.

RELATING TO OTHERS

When we talk about our relational lives, generally we are talking about our loved ones, families, relatives, and even dearest friends. Then when we consider our social lives, we are talking about our neighbors, co-workers, classmates, and other acquaintances we occasionally see and with whom we must get along. You can see, based on the description of the word friend in our previous scripture, that God does not really make that distinction—or does he?

We find in the Bible scriptures like this, **"For there is no respect of persons with God."** (Romans 2:11) So, what does that tell us? To answer that, we need to understand the phrase "no respect of persons" in the Greek is *prosōpolēmpsia* (pronounced pros-o-pol-ape-see'-ah) and means "partiality, favoritism, the fault of one who when called on to give judgment has respect of the outward circumstances of man and not to their intrinsic merits, and so prefers, as the more worthy, one who is rich, high born, or powerful, to another who does not have these qualities."[2] In other words, when God judges someone's actions, he doesn't do it based on the outward display of their lives, but rather on the inward condition of their heart.

Does that mean that God doesn't have favorites? Well, to answer that question, we must define the word favorite. According to the Merriam-Webster dictionary *favorite* means "one that is treated or regarded with special favor or liking; especially: a person who is specially loved, trusted, or provided for."[3] Based on that definition and how we see Jesus treat certain disciples compared to all the others, we would conclude that God does indeed have favorites.

What do I mean? If you recall the story of Jesus's transfiguration upon the mountain in Mark chapter 9, who was with him? Or when he raised the synagogue ruler's daughter from the dead in Mark chapter 5, who were the only ones he allowed into the room with him? Or even when he prayed during his final hours in the garden of Gethsemane in Matthew chapter 26, who were the ones he allowed to be nearest to him at that moment? The answer to these questions is only Peter, James, and John in each case.

You see Jesus had friends (the apostles), then he had close friends (Peter, James, and John), and I believe he even had a best friend (whom I think was John, since he charged him with the care of his mother Mary after his death). There is nothing wrong with that and relationships develop at different levels based on the interest level of each of party.

HOW CLOSE IS CLOSE ENOUGH?

The only difference between us and God, is that while we pick and choose who to become friends with and to what extent, God will invest fully in anyone who wants to be close to him. In other words, anyone can be the best friend of Jesus. How do we know this? Because scripture tells us in James 4:8, **"Draw nigh to God, and he will draw nigh to you."** And recall again Romans 2:11, **"For there is no respect of persons with God."**

The Greek word nigh is *engizō* (pronounced eng-id'-zo)and means "be at hand, come near, or to join one thing to another."4 So, if we come near to God, he will come near to us. If we take a step closer to God, he will take a step closer to us (keep in mind that God's steps are a lot bigger than ours). Remember I pointed out previously the phrase, "respect of persons" in Greek also means favoritism. Hence, God shows no favoritism toward anyone, he will develop as deep of a relationship with you as you want with him.

I often like to say we can have as much of God in our lives as we want or allow. God does not limit himself when we inquire of or pursue him. Just read Hebrews 11:6, **"But without faith it is impossible to please him: for he that cometh to God must believe that he is, and that *he is a rewarder of them that diligently seek him.*"** (Emphasis mine.)

How does God reward those that "diligently seek him?"— with more of himself. We gain greater insight into who God is, how he operates, what he likes and doesn't like. These are the very things we gain as we build relationships with others. The more we open ourselves up to others and expose who we are and what we are about, especially our vulnerabilities, they will be inclined to do the same. This is how our friendships and even our love grows for others, and we bond with them.

ABUNDANCE THROUGH GIVING

This should help us realize that true relational abundance comes not from simply having a large quantity of friends and various relationships, but that those things are a result of our giving ourselves away to others. Hence, there must be something to the response Jesus gave the scribe who wanted to know of God's greatest commandment.

> **And Jesus answered him, "The first of all the commandments is, Hear, O Israel; The Lord our God is one Lord: and thou shalt love the Lord thy God with all thy heart, and with all thy soul, and with all thy mind, and with all thy strength: this is the first commandment. And the second is like, namely this, Thou shalt love thy neighbour as thyself. There is none other commandment greater than these."** (Mark 12:29–30)

You see, these two commandments are blessings in disguise that promise relational abundance, if we will do what they encourage us to do—love God and love others.

Does this mean that everything will always work out and be hunky dory with those we love? Unfortunately, the answer is no. Again, the example is found in Jesus. He literally gave his life away for all those he cared for (and the rest of the world) even when he was rejected and abandoned. In fact, one of his very closest friends, Peter, promised that even if he had to die with Jesus, he would never deny Jesus. Yet, when it came right down to it in the pressure of the moment, he ended up denying him not once, not twice, but three times. Does that mean everything is over—that nothing can be repaired or made whole? We tend to write someone off who has hurt us or abandoned us. But even if it's cliché, we must ask ourselves—what would Jesus do?

Jesus made the first move to reconcile with Peter after Jesus's resurrection. You can read the story of Peter's denial found in John chapter 18 and Jesus's reconciliation with Peter in John chapter 21. I point these out because only in these two stories in the gospels do we find a reference to coal fires. Why is this significant? A coal fire has a very unique and powerful smell. Smell can transport us through space and time. Take a moment to close your eyes and think about someone you love baking something you love.

For me it is sugar cookies my grandmother used to make. When I smell baking sugar cookies I am carried back to when I was a kid waiting for those cookies to come out of the oven so I could enjoy them. Today with the right candle from Bath & Body Works or maybe White Barn I can walk into a room, sniff, and experience that all over again.

Imagine being Peter at the coal fire in chapter 18 and having just denied even knowing his close friend Jesus. Think how disappointed in himself he must have been in that moment, and how he must have thought Jesus would be dissatisfied with him too. Then jump three chapters and several days ahead into the moment when Peter was the first to walk on the beach where Jesus had a coal fire burning. Imagine the scent of the coal fire reaching Peter's nostrils—what did he recall in that moment? Did Jesus need to call him out on it? Did he need Peter to recount and explain himself? No, Jesus simply made a way for Peter to get back on the right track, when he asked him three times if he loved him. Why ask Peter three times? The answer is deep, but the simple explanation is the negative words needed to be offset by positive words offering Peter an opportunity to rebuild or reacknowledge his depth of commitment and love.

Actions always have consequences, but through relational abundance, connections can be restored. Understand it wasn't up to Peter to restore the relationship. Although that would have been ideal, Peter didn't understand relational abundance at the time to do so.

TAKE THE INITIATIVE

We can learn another lesson of relational abundance from Matthew 5:22–24, **"But I say unto you, That whosoever is angry with his brother without a cause shall be in danger of the judgment: and whosoever shall say to his brother, Raca, shall be in danger of the council: but whosoever shall say, Thou fool, shall be in danger of hell fire. Therefore if thou bring thy gift to the altar, and there rememberest *that thy brother hath ought against thee*; leave there thy gift before the altar, and go thy way; first be reconciled to thy brother, and then come and offer thy gift."** (Emphasis mine.)

When someone is hurt, disappointed, or angry with someone else they are depleted of relational abundance. They have drained the relationship of any extra they could give. Notice in this portion of scripture it is not the angry one who is charged with restoring the relationship. Yes, it is the right thing to do, to let go of anger and resentment and to foster healing between parties, but it's not always humanly possible to do so when you are the one who's angry and hurt. Understand, however, it's when you know someone is angry with you, when perhaps you are wrong or even when you have done nothing wrong, that you need to reach out to reconcile the relationship.

Let me say it this way—it's not about you being angry with someone, because in those cases it's obvious we need to make things right. We feel it deep within, prodding us toward reconciliation. This happens because we have a conscience and that's the way God designed it to work. When we do something wrong, our conscience nudges us to go back and correct it. We can either obey it or not, but we cannot deny our responsibility to do so. However, it's in moments when someone is angry with us and we don't have reciprocal feelings, that we are called upon to take the initiative to set things right. This is the demonstration of relational abundance. We go out of our way to help the other person make things right and hopefully resist the urge to hold on to their anger. When we do, it sets both parties free.

Also, notice the word "brother"—we are talking about close relationships in this scripture. Does this hold true for other social relationships? I would say perhaps not because there are differences between our relational lives and our social lives. It may be a lot harder to track down someone we met in a social context to reconcile with them versus someone who is close to us. We will discuss social abundance in the next chapter.

WHEN TO KEEP YOUR MOUTH SHUT

One other thing I want to point out about relational abundance is the simple concept of knowing when and when not to talk. Our culture encourages us to give a response to almost everything, even when we are not directly asked to do so. We should realize not every situation needs our input and not every question needs our answer. Again, we turn to Jesus as our example. When Pilate interrogated Jesus before agreeing to crucify him, we are told in scripture, **"But Jesus yet answered nothing; so that Pilate marvelled."** (Mark 15:5) Sometimes we do more harm than good when we open our mouths. Ecclesiastes 10:12 says, **"The words of a wise man's mouth are gracious; but the lips of a fool will swallow up himself."** So perhaps the wiser thing to do at times is to shut up and listen. I think an anonymous someone got it right when they said, "It's better to keep your mouth shut and appear stupid than to open it and remove all doubt."

When we hold our peace and listen to those who are expressing themselves, we allow them to experience peace through our silence. Maybe this is what is truly meant by the scripture, **"Bear ye one another's burdens, and so fulfil the law of Christ."** (Galatians 6:2) Often, I find the one going through some difficulty and sharing about it just needs me to listen to them. They are disturbed (without peace), and they are having difficulty bearing the situation. But by simply listening to them, I am allowing them to transfer the weight of their concerns to me, so I am bearing the concerns for them in that moment—they can get a breath and experience a bit of peace. This works even when others are upset with you (again see the example of Pilate and Jesus).

This is not possible if you don't have relational abundance. You must have a reserve or an abundance to draw from to be able to give of yourself to someone else. But how do you draw out to give to strangers? That's easy—you build up the relationships you have. An abundance of good relationships keeps us overflowing with kindness and joy, which allows for the giving of ourselves to others. The best way to build up relational abundance is through your spiritual core. When you spend time with God, you build up the spiritual reservoir that can be shared with anyone. You will begin to see yourself the way God sees you. God sees you as someone worth dying for, and that's special. Once you comprehend that, it's easier to begin seeing others in the same light—as someone God loves with an overwhelming love, just as he loves you.

Does that mean you seek to give yourself to everyone no matter what? My answer is a resounding *no*! You must be cautious of toxic relationships. A toxic relationship is one that may be dangerous, destructive, harmful, unsafe, or injurious in any way, whether that's verbal or physical. You can recognize a toxic relationship because it's one that routinely leaves you hurting after your interactions. Typically, toxic people take and take and take some more within the bounds of the relationship and rarely give back. You must do what you can to protect yourself in these relationships and even avoid them if possible.

Once more I will use Jesus as our perfect example. During Jesus's ministry the Pharisees were out to discredit, humiliate, and even harm him. No where do we see Jesus purposefully seeking to share or spend time with them. Instead, we see Jesus was direct and blunt with them. He always spoke the truth in such a way to hopefully open their eyes and motivate them to change. Our interactions in toxic relationships should be the same—to speak truth when spoken to and avoid the relationship altogether if it is hurtful. I would also strongly suggest counseling if you have been in or are currently in a toxic relationship. You need to gain wisdom on how to properly think through the damage the relationship has caused and heal from it. Remember that the way someone else treats you, especially if harmful, is never your fault nor deserved.

You can and should turn to God who can help you with this relationship as he is the ultimate in relational abundance.

TAKE AWAYS

- Relational abundance arises out of the security of our relationships. The more secure we are in ourselves, understanding ourselves, and being all right with ourselves, the greater the capacity we develop for loving others.

- When we give ourselves away to others so they can feel accepted and loved, then we are acting from a place of abundance.

- The relationship we develop with God can emulate the relationships we have with others or vice-versa. If we treat our relationship with God at the same level as the relationships we have with others, then that's all it will ever be, and its impact will be minimal. On the other hand, if we treat it as the most important relationship we have and will ever have and in turn invest everything we are into it, then it will begin to elevate our other relationships in astounding ways.

- God can become our best friend—it depends solely on us and how willing we are to draw close to him.

- We are charged with the responsibility to help repair damaged relationships. We must allow relational abundance to move us to take the initiative—even when we are in the right—to help reconcile with someone who feels they've been wronged.

- An important aspect of relational abundance is knowing when and when not to talk. When we give someone else the space to unburden themselves without judgment and recommendations, they can experience a moment of peace and be impacted by the generosity of the relationship.

- Toxic relationships are poisonous to our existence. We must avoid the poison that drains us of energy and of ourselves. We must speak the harsh truth to those who are toxic to us in hopes they will change. We must also seek assistance for ourselves if we've been damaged by these relationships to find restoration and healing.

- Relational abundance can only flow from a well that is full. We must periodically be filling our own well through an abundance of positive, sustaining relationships we maintain with others. The most important source of filling of our tank is God. That is the one relationship that will keep fulfilling our need for proper perspective and love.

NEXT STEPS

Take stock for a moment of your relationships. I'm talking about more than your social interactions. I'm talking about those you consider close to you. Are you a source of relational abundance for them? Are they a source of abundance for you? Think about how you can take the initiative and offer reconciliation to any of those relationships that are or have been suffering. If you're not sure how or where to start, take it to God in prayer and ask for guidance. Let the relationship you have with your great Creator pour into you the abundance necessary for you to be able to pour into others.

Assess the type of relationship you have with God. Be honest about it. Is it what you think it should be? Do you think your relationship with God could be improved? If so, remember God is not holding himself back from you.

Therefore, are you willing to commit your all to God in your relationship with him? If not, what is holding you back? Tell him about that and let him help you resolve it. Do you want your relationship with God to be the number one relationship you have? If so, I believe it can be. You and God can be BFF's, just commit to confiding in and sharing your thoughts, hurts, hopes, dreams, everything with him—and then be sure to close your mouth and allow him to speak to you. I believe you will find not only are you loved more that you could imagine, but that there is an abundance flowing in and through you to others that only comes from him.

TRANSITION

Since we've begun the discussion on relational abundance, we must logically continue by addressing social abundance. Together they make up the entire area of all human interactions. You can't have abundance in one area without having abundance in the other or you'd be out of balance. And if you recall, true abundance only comes from being in proper balance as it relates to our core and the outflow of it into every area of our lives. Therefore, let's jump into the next chapter and learn about true social abundance from God's viewpoint.

10
SOCIAL ABUNDANCE

"Human beings are social creatures. We are social not just in the trivial sense that we like company, and not just in the obvious sense that we each depend on others. We are social in a more elemental way: simply to exist as a normal human being requires interaction with other people."

–ATUL GAWANDE

"**S**WEETIE, I HAVE TO GO."

"But I don't want you to go," she cried, tears welling up in her little, beautiful brown eyes as she looked up at me.

It was breaking my heart because everything within me wanted to stay with her as much as she wanted me to stay. I hugged her tight and resisted the overwhelming urge to pick her up in my arms and carry her away with me.

"It's going to be all right. I'm going to see you later tonight, but for now I have to go to work."

I wasn't sure any of this was registering in a four-year-old's mind especially since she was resisting and insisting that I stay.

"It's typical separation anxiety," the nice lady at the door said to me.

She had seen it thousands of times before which made her immune to it, but for me experiencing it for the first time, it made me swallow my heart as it crept up into my throat. I was dropping off my daughter for her first day of preschool. For some it's uneventful, but it felt very traumatic for my daughter and me. And it still feels that way for me as I relive the experience (as I write this, tears overcome me—I'll explain why in just a bit). I knew deep in my heart preschool would benefit her and be a blessing to both of us in the long run, but in the moment, it was very difficult.

If we pause for a minute and think about it, we all have some form of separation anxiety. Most of us are anxious when we are called to step out of our comfort zone and do something new. We'd rather cling to the familiar than dive into the unknown. Many use the phrase, "the devil we know is better than the devil we don't know" to justify a stay-put decision. I think this is a horrible phrase because if I'm hanging out with a devil, whether known or not, then I'm keeping the wrong company and should actively be looking for a change. Social abundance cannot come from anxiousness, which is another word for fear, and it certainly can't come from holding back. We must be willing to separate ourselves from our fears to experience true social abundance.

OVERCOME THE FEAR

They say the number one fear of people, even above the fear of dying, is public speaking. I believe that's because it's usually done in front of strangers. And offering a part of yourself to someone you don't know, in any social situation is always a little unnerving and traumatic. I believe it's because we don't know how they will react to our interaction. And this fear is derived from the sense that we are responsible for their reaction.

Here's the key to set you free—you're not responsible for how someone else chooses to react! If we can fully understand that, then there should be nothing that fear can do to us. There should no longer be a reason to hold back.

The reason my eyes leaked, as I mentioned a moment ago, was because as I remembered dropping my daughter off for preschool, I envisioned that this is how God feels each time he places one of his innocent, tender, dearest creations into the world. He knows they are going to encounter social situations beneficial for them in the long run but that can be very difficult and awkward in the moment. Just read John chapter 14 (to me it almost sounds like a father dropping his kids off at preschool), and you'll understand what I am saying.

Within that chapter we are encouraged by Jesus with his words, **"I will not leave you comfortless: I will come to you"** (John 14:18), and **"Peace I leave with you, my peace I give unto you: not as the world giveth, give I unto you. Let not your heart be troubled, neither let it be afraid."** (John 14:27)

God knows we are going to encounter some things that will require us to be comforted and other things that will seem to take our peace away in this world. So, he reassures us—as I did with my daughter, letting her know things would not stay like that. There is always a purpose for what we go through, and it will be all right. We can *know* we are not alone. God is always with us.

THIS TOO SHALL PASS

Not much in life is guaranteed, but there is one thing we can count on—change. No matter how life is now, it is not going to stay that way. That's why one of my favorite expressions in scripture is the phrase, "it came to pass." This common phrase is found throughout the Bible well over 400 times. God deliberately used this phrase when starting a story or sharing a thought to communicate something to us. I believe God wanted to teach us that things in this life come and go with great frequency, but the key is in the verbiage. You see he was saying that things come to "pass," they don't come to stay. I believe if we understand this idea, then we can both plan and be comforted with it. We can plan when things are good because we know they won't always stay that way—so we appreciate them when we have them. We gather during the good seasons and plan for when they turn on us. We are also comforted when things are not so good because this phrase reminds us, we don't have to live here. Things will improve. Something good will come along in God's timing. The key is to remember who is in charge, and when we trust God, we know that no matter what, he's working on our behalf to make us the best version of ourselves that we can be.

And we know that *all things* work together for good to them that love God, to them who are the called according to his purpose. (Romans 8:28) (Emphasis mine.)

Once we were saved, we may wish that God would take us out of this world to reside with him in heaven and thereby avoid all temptation and evil here on this earth. However, God has other plans for us. He wants us to have social abundance.

How can we have social abundance? Well, if relational abundance only comes from giving oneself away to others, then social abundance must be similar. However, there are also differences in our relational lives versus social lives.

HOW'S OUR INTIMACY?

The first difference between our relational and social lives is the level of intimacy we have in our relationships and the types of interactions we have, because of that intimacy. When we know someone, we say we have a relationship with them. Depending on how much we know about them and how much they know about us, we can gauge the level of intimacy we have with them. Hence, both relationships and social contacts register as interactions, but relationships tend to be longer, deeper, and more meaningful. Our interactions give us the opportunity to look deep within at who we are as individuals and for us to open up and expose our true selves to others. We learn more about who we are through close relationships and when we know ourselves well it becomes easier to share ourselves.

On the other hand, in social interactions with people we know very little if anything about, our purpose is to overcome fear, take risks, compare direction, and obtain general guidance. These interactions also allow us to solidify and prove what we have discovered about ourselves from our other relationships. For example, when in a social setting where people are not known on a very deep level, we can interact and discover what it is they do, how they operate in certain ways, and a little bit about what they might believe. Then we can ascertain if we want to move in the same direction with them or not.

Take the typical high school freshman, who is trying to discover who they want to be. They observe and interact with the various cliques or circles already established within the school setting. They might take notice of the sports jocks, the nerds who are into learning and techy things, the popular crowd who are into fashion and trends, or even the fine arts geeks—those who are into art, music, and performance. They might try some activities or clubs with these various crowds to see if their habits, behaviors, and beliefs feel comfortable enough to participate further and if so, they slowly begin to adapt as one of them.

WE ARE HERE TO SHARE

God doesn't usually take us home to be with him immediately after we've been saved. He wants us to interact with others and share this new experience of salvation with them. He allows this time of sharing to prove to us the truth of our experience and provide an example for others to follow and discover him for themselves. This is called evangelism, witnessing, or simply living the life of a believer.

God wants us to share him with others! Hence, while social abundance comes from the giving away of ourselves, as I stated before, it is what we share that is different. In both types of interactions (relational or social), we share God, especially if he is at the core of our being, as he should be. However, with relational interactions the focus is more about sharing who he has made us to be or sharing the depth of who we are in him. In social interactions though, it's more about sharing who he is with others and what he can do in them.

You see, when Jesus said to Peter and his brother Andrew, **"Follow me, and I will make you fishers of men"** (Matthew 4:19), he was in essence saying I'm going to use who you are to share me with others. They were both fishermen. That was their occupation; however, I believe it was also who they were deep within. Having known some professional fishermen in my life (my grandfather was a commercial fisherman on Lake Superior in Washburn, Wisconsin), I can imagine them talking deeply about bait, lures, nets, kinds of fish, boats, lines, the best hours and spots to fish, the best way to fillet a fish, and so on.

Although Jesus changed them (their preferences, attitudes, decision making process, etc.) through the relationship he developed with them over three and half years, it did not change the essence of who they were. They were still simple fishermen. We see that because after his death, the first thing they did was return to fishing. However, we also see the powerful effect of their witnessing, as multitudes were drawn to Christ because of their example.

> **Now when they saw the boldness of Peter and John, and perceived that *they were unlearned and ignorant men*, they marvelled; and they took knowledge of them, *that they had been with Jesus.* (Acts 4:13) (Emphasis mine.)**

We see two things in this scripture, one being the proof that others saw something in Peter and John that convinced them that the apostles knew Jesus; and two, there was boldness in them. That means the lack of fear. Therefore, social abundance cannot be derived from fear.

DO IT BRAVELY

When there is fear in a social setting, one tends to withdraw and close oneself off for protection. This means that social abundance can only be accompanied by boldness or bravery, which is an act that overcomes fear. You may have heard the phrase, "feel the fear and do it anyway." This phrase has helped me numerous times to overcome things that initially caused apprehension. Exercising courage and doing what I was apprehensive about provided me the experience to overcome fear much easier the next time until I no longer experience fear—or at least not to the point that it immobilizes me. Public speaking and singing in front of others are my personal examples. I can successfully do both now without fear causing my arms to go numb or my mouth to become as dry as the Arizona desert, both of which used to be very inconvenient.

For God hath not given us the spirit of fear; but of power, and of love, and of a sound mind. (2 Timothy 1:7)

I used this scripture previously when we talked about mental abundance, but it's worth the reminder that fear doesn't come from God. Therefore, fear must derive itself from the enemy as one of his weapons. Knowing this we can also rely upon this scripture, **"No weapon that is formed against thee shall prosper."** (Isaiah 54:17) Perhaps this is also why scripture tells us at least 365 times (one for every day of the year) not to fear or for us to resist fear.

Does simply resisting fear and displaying courage mean that we are going to be successful in every social interaction to testify of the goodness of God? I wish that were the case, but not every social situation is going to be filled with people who will come to like us. We may face social situations with people we would call our enemies because of the way they treat us or interact with us. What do we do in those cases? How are we to still have social abundance in those situations?

Therefore if thine enemy hunger, feed him; if he thirst, give him drink: for in so doing thou shalt heap coals of fire on his head. (Romans 12:20)

LOVING OUR ENEMIES

You might read this and think, *Ah ha, there it is. We show kindness to our enemies to destroy them, because it's right there in the words, "heap coals of fire on his head."* But you would be wrong. In the days that the apostle Paul wrote this, it was commonplace for middle easterners to show this kindness to their guests. When visitors stayed long into the evening and the sun had gone down, the temperatures would drop. As the visitors left, they would face the cold of the night on their journey home. Therefore, their host would take some warm embers or coals from the fire, wrap them up well, and place them on their visitor's heads, which would help keep them warm on their way back home.

So, Paul's words are encouraging us to show kindness even to those that are against us—and not just an ordinary convenient kindness but a go-out-of-your-way-to-handle-something-that-may-even-hurt-a-bit type of kindness for the benefit of others (pulling coals out of a fire and wrapping them up definitely is not convenient, nor is it without some risk to the one performing the task). This type of kindness demonstrates social abundance and the giving of ourselves away even to those who don't deserve it. In fact, these types of gestures cannot come from anywhere else but a place of abundance. If we give this kind of love only to those whom we love or even those we may like, there is really no abundance demonstrated as there is enough provision to allow for those who can return the favor. But by giving yourself in social situations where there is no possibility of reciprocation, then it must be done from the abundance flowing from one's heart.

For if ye love them which love you, what thank have ye? for sinners also love those that love them. (Luke 6:32)

We must be willing to give of ourselves to others in the hope that the kindness we show will point them to the one who is always full of kindness for them. The kindness God shows is evident in providing for everyone's needs, even through the provision of sunshine and rain to help nurture and allow for growth—since even those who do not yet acknowledge him or his acts of kindness benefit from them.

> **That ye may be the children of your Father which is in heaven: for he maketh his sun to rise on the evil and on the good, and sendeth rain on the just and on the unjust.** (Matthew 5:45)

It can seem overwhelming for an introvert to be able to give of themselves, especially in extroverted settings like parties or large group activities. In those cases, you may need to heed the previous advice of, "feel the fear and do it anyway," or better yet you may need to look for one-on-one social situations that allow you to share God with others. Remember God can use the essence of who you are to the utmost and can create opportunities for you to experience the joy of social abundance even in very small doses.

One thing holds true, however, for introverts and extroverts. Interactions are unavoidable. We cannot avoid being around other people. They are everywhere we go—in the grocery store, at the dentist office, when driving down the road, or even working from home. We have more than enough chances throughout the day to encounter another human being, whether on the phone, a Zoom call, an email, text message, or even face-to-face. Therefore as scripture instructs us, we should be ready to interact at any moment and share God's goodness with others.

> **But sanctify the Lord God in your hearts: and be ready always to give an answer to every man that asketh you a reason of the hope that is in you with meekness and fear.** (1 Peter 3:15)

TAKE AWAYS

- We all face some form of separation anxiety. We must separate ourselves from our comfort zone and embrace new opportunities to interact with others to experience true social abundance.

- We are not responsible for how someone chooses to react to us. We must do what is right in any situation and do our best—that is called controlling ourselves—but that's the extent of our control. Controlling ourselves is difficult enough without thinking we must control how others respond.

- God knows we are going to have difficult social encounters, but he promises us we are not alone. He is always with us, willing to help us through them. He allows them so that through them we will grow and experience the abundance he desires for us.

- There is only one guarantee in life, and that is change. We will all experience change on a regular basis. Since we know this, we can better prepare when things are good and take heart when things are bad.

- God wants us to experience relational and social abundance to develop intimacy and a willingness to share. When we know ourselves, we can share with ease.

- Sharing God with others in hope that they too can experience his kindness is the entire reason God doesn't take us to heaven to be with him the moment we are saved.

- Fear doesn't come from God. It's a weapon of the enemy and since God promises that no weapon formed against a believer shall prosper, we don't have to succumb to fear.

- Social abundance can only be experienced when we are willing to give of ourselves—even to those whom we may call enemies.

- Interactions with others are unavoidable, so we need to be ready at all times to share with them about God's goodness.

NEXT STEPS

Is something hindering you from experiencing social abundance? Have you been hesitant to tell others how God has blessed you? Has fear stopped you? If so, can you identify the fear? Is it the fear of embarrassing yourself? Is it the fear of needing others to like you? Is it the fear of failure? Remember the only opinion of you that truly matters is God's—and God thinks you are incredible! He loves you beyond words. His love was proved by his actions—going to the cross to die for you so you could be with him in eternity. If this is how God feels about you then does anybody else's opinion of you really matter?

Fear is a weapon the enemy uses to keep you from experiencing abundance. Recall that scripture says no weapon formed against you shall prosper or succeed. Therefore, Satan's weapon is already flawed and weak. That's why we can easily say faith is greater than fear. When you trust

God, you have all the power of heaven backing you and there is no way you will fail.

Take some time in prayer and let God know what fears the enemy has been trying out against you and then claim in faith that God will destroy those fears and equip you with courage to conquer them. I believe you will experience greater abundance than you could ever imagine. It all starts when you are willing to share what God has done for you with others.

TRANSITION

We are over halfway through our mnemonic of M.I.G.H.T. with only two more areas to cover. Our learning muscles are being developed and we are ready to grasp the final trainings. Now is not the time to turn back, we must continue to exercise and build upon our knowledge. I trust that you won't break a sweat as we get into discussing physical abundance in the next chapter.

11
PHYSICAL ABUNDANCE

And he said unto them, "Take heed, and beware of
covetousness: for a man's life consisteth not in the
abundance of the things which he possesseth."
–LUKE 12:15

STRONGLY DEBATED WHAT I should call this chapter. I tossed
around ideas like Health in Abundance, Abundant Health,
Physical Health and Abundance, with each one containing
the word health. As you can see, I settled on the title Physical
Abundance. Still, I was concerned about this title because I
was afraid some might think I was talking about the surplus
of things—physical stuff (I'll touch on that in the next chapter when it comes to finances). The struggle was real for me
because I didn't want people to think I was talking about
material goods, but if I used the word health I didn't want to
limit our discussion on abundance to feeling good. So, when
I decided to use my current title, I also decided to open with
the scripture quote above to emphasize that our life on earth
is not entirely made up of the things we own.

We all can get swept up in materialism and forget the source
of our joy. Even when we recall that life is not made up of our
things, we tend to think it's about how we feel physically. After
all, if the commercials on TV, the internet, and in magazines
are not pumping out promises to feel great once you own this

or that, then they are driving us to lose weight, take medicine, or eat or drink something to feel great physically.

A TIME OF HEALING

You have understood by now that in the mnemonic device of the word M.I.G.H.T. the letter H stands for health and God does want abundance of health for us. But what does that truly mean. That's what I want to dive into here, so let me share a story:

We were running terribly late, with a baby and all the necessary supplies (diaper bag, toys, snacks, pacifier, etc.) in our arms. We rushed into the evening church service that had already started and quickly found our spot in the back pew. We had been routinely sitting in the back of the church since attending so that our little bundle of joy wouldn't steal anyone else's joy during the sermons.

Just as we set down our things, I heard the pastor call for prayer for someone in the church. That person was standing in the front and people were gathering around him to pray. In our hurry and commotion, I missed it when the pastor said who we were praying for. Having been at the church for less than a year, I didn't recognize him as anyone I had talked to up to that point. Still, I felt an overwhelming tug in my spirit to join the others and pray for him. I told my wife I was going up to pray and left her holding our little girl.

When I reached the front, several people were laying hands upon the young man and praying feverishly. I learned God wants us to exercise authority in prayer and one way to do so is to face a situation head on, so I decided to stand right in front of him to pray. As I did, I felt led to place my hand upon his throat and pray. When I placed my hand on the side of his throat, I felt a lump about the size of a golf ball. We all prayed for a while (I'm guessing it was no more than a few minutes), but as we prayed, I felt the lump disappear. It was odd—I had never experienced anything like that. I didn't even know for what we were praying. I thought maybe I was imagining it because nobody said anything, and the young man didn't react. We finished praying and the service continued. I returned to my seat to join my wife.

About a week later in the morning service the pastor asked the same young man to stand up and share something. Danny (now I learned his name) said he had been struggling with the news the doctors had given him and during the past week he was supposed to have surgery on the cancer in his throat. However, after the congregation prayed for him, it had disappeared. He went to the doctor during the week who confirmed it—no more cancer. The place exploded with excitement, and I knew I had been part of a miracle God had done.

Was it because of me or my prayer? I highly doubt it—after all I hadn't even known why we were praying. But I witnessed what someone's prayer of faith allowed God to do for Danny, and it was an incredible blessing! I want you to understand that God indeed wants you to experience physical abundance in your health.

We know God is a compassionate God and when he walked this earth in the physical form we know as Jesus, he healed all those who came to him and sought him out. He even healed those who didn't directly ask him—like the widow's son whom he raised from the dead without asking her permission first (read Luke 7:12-15). We're told he simply did it out of compassion.

A GREATER PURPOSE

There are times when I've had a need, asked God, and he healed me. But there have been other times when I've had a need and asked God for healing, and I haven't received it. What was different about those times? I'm not sure anything was different, so why didn't this compassionate God heal me as I thought he should? Perhaps those were times I was to learn what Paul did when he asked God over and over for his prayer to be answered, **"And he said unto me, 'My grace is sufficient for thee: for my strength is made perfect in weakness'."** (2 Corinthians 12:9)

So, does physical abundance mean that we are going to always be healthy? I think based on this scripture quote we can clearly see that is not the case. While it may be God's desire for us to be healthy, he has a greater purpose for physical abundance. Physical abundance truly is allowing God to work through our physical bodies as he so chooses. Remember everything in our lives derives or flows outward from the core we establish in our lives. If we've established the right spiritual core, then central to everything we do is God. This must also be true when considering our physical bodies.

> **And as Jesus passed by, he saw a man which was blind from his birth. And his disciples asked him, saying, Master, who did sin, this man, or his parents, that he was born blind? Jesus answered, "Neither hath this man sinned, nor his parents:** *but that the works of God should be made manifest in him.***"** (John 9:1–3) (Emphasis mine.)

We see based on this scripture that the man's health issue was allowed by God because God was going to use it to show his might. However, if we keep reading this account in scripture, we will see that Jesus healed this man of his blindness, but the reason was to show the condition of the hearts of the Pharisees. This man's healing distressed and agitated them, but it also allowed those previously under the influence of the Pharisees to see the truth and power of God.

I was away on business in Amarillo, Texas for several weeks. One evening as I was finishing work, my heart began palpitating quite strongly. Palpitations were nothing new to me as I had been having them ever since I was a teenager and had been on medication for them for several years as an adult. Had these palpitations been like others I wouldn't have thought twice about it and would have brushed it off. However, these were different—they felt stronger and more urgent. I tried several things to try to get them under control, but nothing was working, and I was getting concerned and a little lightheaded.

I'll admit I can be a big baby. I faint at the sight of blood and can even faint at the strong thought of blood. Knowing this about myself, I wondered if maybe I was making more of this than I should. So, I called my wife back in Wisconsin. She is a cardiac rehab supervising nurse who has worked with heart related issues, even open-heart surgery patients, for years. She also knew about my palpitations, so I thought she would give me some good advice. After talking with her, I decided to go to the emergency room just to be on the safe side. Being the big baby I am, I don't like hospitals and I *really* don't like needles, so agreeing to go to the emergency room meant these palpitations were significant.

When I told the front desk nurse why I was there, they issued me into a room right away. Hospitals don't waste time on heart issues in case someone is having a heart attack. Immediately a nurse came in and began trying to get an I.V. in me. I clearly knew she was new when after five needle pricks, she still was unsuccessful—and that did not sit well with someone who hates needles. As she was preparing for her sixth attempt, another nurse stepped in and took over. Her name tag said she was Julie, my wife's name, so we started some small talk. After a couple of minutes, God revealed something to me about Julie. I asked her something like do you have such and such going on in your life? She stopped what she was doing, looked at me with a slack jaw expression, and asked how I knew that. I answered that God told me and as soon as I did, God started speaking to Julie through me and we prayed together. As soon as we finished praying, my palpitations ceased, and I felt normal. I was discharged and my next few weeks in Amarillo were uneventful.

I share this story to show you that God can use our health or even what seems like the lack thereof for his purposes, which are always greater than our own. Therefore, having physical abundance does not strictly mean having perfect physical health. As, I've mentioned many times before, abundance only comes once you have enough to meet your own needs and the excess can be shared with others. When we have confidence that God will take care of our physical health either by healing us directly or using our situation for his purposes, then we have more than we need—we have abundance. How can I prove it biblically?

And Moses was an hundred and twenty years old when he died: his eye was not dim, nor his natural force abated. (Deuteronomy 34:7)

IT'S ABOUT WHAT GOD CAN DO

Now think about this, Moses was 120 years old. Even if you-adjust that for the difference between our current calendar year and the Hebrew biblical calendar (the Hebrew biblical year is only 360 days) that means he was still over 118 years old. That's old! How many 118-year-olds, if you can find them, don't have some health issues? You may understand Moses didn't have any health issues based on this scripture, but is that really what it's saying to us? To know for sure, we must understand the Hebrew for the phrase "his eye" which comes from the Hebrew *'ayin* (pronounced ah'-yin) and not only means "eye" but also means "as showing mental qualities and of mental and spiritual faculties."[1] So, what does that tell us? I believe that this scripture is focused more on the fact that Moses's mind was still clear and that he still had a very good grasp of God.

What does the other phrase "his natural force" mean? The Hebrew word for this is *lēaḥ* (pronounced lay'-akh) and means "freshness or vigor."[2] We might refer to this as stamina, strength or better yet energy. Have you seen some old people that although wrinkly and feeble still have a lot of "get-up-and-go" in them? It doesn't mean they don't have aches and pains; it just means they don't let those aches and pains stop them. I think this is the essence of what this phrase is trying to tell us. Also consider that the word "abated" in Hebrew is *nûs* (pronounced noos) and means "to subside, flee away, take flight, or depart."[3] Hence, I believe that physical abundance means having enough energy or stamina to continuously answer the call of God for whatever he wants to do and accomplish physically through you for the sake of others.

Here's one more reason I believe that. When I read through the histories of the Jewish people as written by Flavius Josephus, who was a Jewish historian during the time of Jesus, he told the story of God meeting with the Israelites on Mount Sinai just after bringing them out of Egypt (see Exodus chapters 19 and

20). In his description of the account, he used an interesting word to describe when God spoke to them or rather *how* he spoke to them. He utilized the word energy rather than using a word like importance or severity[4]. To me, by use of this word he was implying something about the nature of God, that God is energy.

This led me to study energy, and it's interesting to know that we measure energy in frequency or waves (This is greatly simplified so I could understand and communicate it). There are basically seven types of energy waves: radio waves, microwaves, infrared, optical (visible light), ultraviolet radiation, x-rays, and gamma rays. However, there are certain waves that can only be studied in space due to their energy levels. Why does this matter or why is this important? Think of it this way: when the ocean waves crash, they release a lot of energy, but where did that energy originate? I know scientists can give a very educated sounding answer but I'm trying to be very basic here. If we believe God is in and through everything, that means that energy came from God.

Recall in chapter eight I referred to what Einstein said about energy—it can't be created or destroyed, only changed or transferred. I believe he was meaning in this physical world. In this realm Einstein is correct, energy cannot be created or destroyed because energy is not something that was created along with other physical things. If energy cannot be created in our physical world, it had to have come from somewhere for it to exist here in the physical. I believe it came directly from God. When he created this world, he put part of himself into it, just like he put a part of himself into man when God created him (hence why it can't be destroyed since something physical cannot destroy something supernatural). Look again at man's origins when God breathed into man the breath of life, and he became a living soul—in other words he had the energy needed to sustain life. Where did that energy come from? God! To overly simplify then, we could say God is pure energy. The purest, highest form of energy.

So the application is this, when we have God as our core—the very center of our lives—he will give us the proper level of energy needed to carry out our tasks for his glory regardless of our physical shape. Look at Nick Vujicic who was born without limbs but changes countless lives by preaching the gospel around the world.

A PROPER PERSEPCTIVE

When new agers focus on energy as God and try to harness that energy through crystals or whatever, they are missing it. Yes, God is pure energy, but he is so much more than that. When you only focus on one part of God rather than trying to comprehend his other qualities you wind up in idol worship, which God hates.

Read about the Israelites in Exodus chapter 32, when they came out of Egypt and Moses went up the mountain for forty days and nights to receive the ten commandments. The people back in the camp wanted to celebrate God and have God lead them but Moses was gone a long time and they thought he wasn't coming back. They pressured Aaron to fashion a bull out of their gold earrings and other gold items they melted. They then worshiped this bull and declared it was what brought them out of Egypt. Now surely, they knew a bull didn't bring them out of Egypt but rather they looked to the strength of God—like the strength of a bull—that brought them out of Egypt. They saw one aspect of God, his strength, and they worshiped only that. When they did so, they got off kilter doing things they shouldn't have been doing, which displeased God because those things went against another characteristic of God—purity. God wants to be appreciated for his entirety, just as we do in our relationships. I don't want my wife to only see me as a provider. I want her to appreciate me as a creative, loving, fun person and as everything else that makes me who I am. Sure, God is vast and beyond our human understanding, but he has shown us who he is through his word the Bible so we can grasp the important parts of his character.

God is a healer as we see throughout scripture, but that is not the source of our physical abundance. It is incredible when he heals us and we should pray that he does, but in those moments when we don't gain our healing, we should trust that God has a greater purpose. The abundance that comes through the sufficiency of his grace operating through us, even though we may be experiencing weakness, is more than enough to accomplish the tasks we are given. It is more than enough to keep us going and serving our great Creator, so that others will say of us like they did of Moses, their minds were clear, their hearts were right, and the energy of God flows through them.

SOME PRACTICALITIES

What are some practical things you can do in your life to create physical abundance? Even those who don't live for God, know the importance of eating healthy by eliminating or reducing the amount of chemicals they put into their bodies. The old adage, "you are what you eat" has a lot of truth to it. We sometimes wonder why we feel sluggish and tired, yet we have put heavy sludge into our engine and question why it's not firing on all cylinders. If we will discipline ourselves to eat right, our bodies will begin to feel good and operate better.

Getting proper rest is important as well. We all know how refreshing it is to get a good night's sleep after we have gone through a long period of not sleeping well. However, there should be no reason we can't obtain a good night's sleep every night or at least increase the number of good nights. By establishing a sleep routine to get ourselves prepared to sleep, we can increase our chances for a good night's rest. This allows our mind to slow down and recognize that it is time to relax. Of course, you will have to find what works for you through trial and error. With today's wearable devices, like smart watches, we can also review our sleep patterns and get a better feel for what's working. However, rest isn't all about sleep, sometimes it's simply that—rest. Instead of pushing ourselves to go, go, go to get as much done as possible, we may need to slow down and realize that work will still be there tomorrow, the dishes can wait until the next day, or that even if we kill ourselves due to exhaustion, the world is still going to continue. God has provided us the gift of rest and why would we reject it? It all comes down to balance and finding the right mix for our energy levels.

Lastly, we all know the importance of exercise. Getting some exercise is better than none and getting more exercise is better than getting just some. There is a definite payoff between how much we exercise and how good we look and feel. For most of us though, we must balance it with all our other responsibilities. Just twenty minutes a day of exercise can improve both your physical health and your mental mood. It shouldn't be difficult to work into our daily routines. We must establish a routine or discipline with regular exercise.

When we do, it becomes second nature to us, and we tend to resist it less.

Doing these things will help us keep our temple in good habitable condition for God to work in and through our lives. It shows God that we desire him to work in us by us doing our part and trusting him to do his part.

In conclusion, we must keep in mind that we have a responsibility as directed in scripture to take care of our body that was given to us by God. **"What? know ye not that your body is the temple of the Holy Ghost which is in you, which ye have of God, and ye are not your own? For ye are bought with a price: therefore glorify God in your body, and in your spirit, which are God's."** (1 Corinthians 6:19–20)

This scripture clearly emphasizes that it's up to us to care for and treat this body correctly so God can move through us to accomplish his purposes, which will bring him glory. Therefore, if we are overweight, slothful, or mistreating our body with abusive chemicals (yes, caffeine is a chemical too and can be abused), not getting enough sleep, or eating the wrong things, are we treating our bodies correctly? God doesn't expect perfection, but that does not give us license to neglect his gift of our physical form. We must do what we can to eat right, exercise, and get the rest we need as we attempt to keep the other areas of our lives in balance. We must use caution here too, so we don't take the maintenance of our bodies to the extreme and get so caught up in working out or eating clean that it becomes an idol for us, and we lose our focus on the why—that God is to be glorified. In other words, we don't want to only beautify the temple and forget about the one to be worshiped residing within who is even more glorious.

TAKE AWAYS

- Physical abundance has to do with our health, not the accumulation of things. Even then it's not entirely about how we feel physically, but it's more about how God can move through our lives and use us physically to accomplish his purposes.

- God wants us to be healthy and can heal us when we are not, all it requires is faith and simply asking him. This is how miracles happen.

- God can even use our times of physical distress for the purpose of reaching others. When we are open to and willing for God to use us in this way, our physical ailments can be less taxing on us. Often God will restore us when his purpose has been accomplished.

- Physical abundance means having enough energy and/or stamina to continuously answer the call of God for what he wants to do and accomplish physically through you for the sake of others.

- We must maintain the proper perspective of our physical existence. While we must strive to take good care of the body with which we have been blessed, we also need to avoid allowing it to become an idol. The same goes even for those with physical ailments that God uses for his glory—we must not get caught up in the accolades of how God uses us or forget that the purpose is to bring him glory, not self-notoriety.

NEXT STEPS

How have you been treating your body? Have you given it the proper care it needs to show God you appreciate his gift of life? If your temple is in disarray, you can take some initiative to spruce it up. I'm not talking about simple appearance issues like applying some make-up or getting a new hair style. I'm talking about eating right, exercising, and getting some rest. Pray about what changes you can make, remember you are only responsible for what you can do, and ask God to do the rest. If that's only going for a walk down the block today because that's all the energy you have, then do it and pray that God will help you run marathons in the future, for example.

If your body has suffered the effects of some difficult living and you need healing, then ask God and trust that he desires to and can heal you. If healing is not instantaneous, then trust he will lead you down the right path to obtain your healing. Read scriptures about healing and learn what it means to have faith. The Gospels are full of stories and events where Jesus healed individuals because of their faith or the faith of others. So, if your faith is low, ask others to join you in prayer for your healing.

Lastly, if you've prayed about healing but it hasn't come yet, then ask God how he desires to use your physical condition to reach others. Be open to the idea that God can move through you and your situation to be a blessing to someone else. As you give your situation to him for his purposes, remember, **"God loveth a cheerful giver"** (2 Corinthians 9:7b), so do your best to maintain a good attitude and outlook throughout your period of physical ailment. If you need an attitude adjustment toward your physical limitations, take it to God in prayer and ask him to help you become cheerful even in your distress. I know it's not easy, but he can turn all things around and perhaps that's what he's been waiting for before touching you.

TRANSITION

We are almost through our mnemonic M.I.G.H.T., just one more topic to go! In the next chapter we are going to talk about T, our treasury. You might be surprised by how God views financial abundance so let's get ready for some great discovery.

12
FINANCIAL ABUNDANCE

*"Money never made a man happy yet, nor will it.
The more a man has, the more he wants.
Instead of filling a vacuum, it makes one."*
–Benjamin Franklin

I COULDN'T HELP MYSELF. I felt as though I lost all control of my body and I slumped to the floor. As I did, I cried out to God for help. I held my head in my hands, sobbing. I was overwhelmed, stressed, and shell-shocked.

It was toward the end of the day, on a Saturday, and I had just opened the mail—nothing unusual about that. However, I was hit with another bill. It was a routine utility bill but it was much higher than usual—it was 200 dollars. That may not seem like enough to drop me to the floor, but this was also almost thirty years ago when our average utility bill was closer to seventy-five dollars for our two-bedroom apartment. Additionally, I had been unemployed for almost thirteen months and our resources were depleted.

Financial distress was not a fun way to start a marriage. We were married in September of 1994, and I changed jobs in March of 1995. I thought it was a great opportunity for growth. However, largely due to circumstances beyond my control, I was let go by June. I landed a new job within a month, in a new field because I didn't really like my accounting profession, so I wanted to try something different.

Unfortunately, that job was not a good fit and within the month we mutually agreed to part ways, which then led me to being unemployed for thirteen months. Being out of work that long was mostly my fault because I was trying to find a more satisfying career path.

My adopted dad was an accountant and I saw what a good lifestyle it offered. Since I had taken an accounting course my senior year in high school and easily aced it, I thought, *OK, I can do this and then go back for music.* My parents said they were not going to pay for me to get a music degree, which is what I truly wanted to do. Actually, they ended up only loaning me the money to attend school, which I repaid, so perhaps I should have studied music originally. (It's obvious now looking back God had a different plan.)

Now here I was almost five years out of college, and there didn't seem to be the right opportunity for me to go back for music nor were there any funds to allow it, especially not since I was a married man. I was desperately trying to find something that would allow me to earn a good living but also express my creative side. Hence the thirteen months.

As I said earlier, when I saw that bill and thought about all the others we had with nothing left to cover them, I broke. When you hear that someone is broke, you think of them being out of money and that's correct, but it's more. It's when they are not only out of money, but also out of hope. That was nearly me. I say nearly because my only thread of hope was that God would somehow take care of us.

At the time I was too blind to see the many ways God took care of us. We were living on spaghetti almost every night plus some things from the church's food pantry, a ministry the church *started* during the time I was out of work—talk about God's perfect timing! Hopefully, I've painted a clear enough picture of how bleak I thought our situation was, because that's how I felt. And so, I sat there on the floor crying out to God. My wife came over, hugged me, and we prayed together. Praying made me feel somewhat better, and we moved on for the remainder of the night.

AN ANSWER TO PRAYER

The next morning, when we walked in the door at church, I greeted a friend of mine who had a big smile on his face. He walked directly over to me, grabbed my hand as to shake it, but pulled me close into a hug and whispered in my ear that in prayer last night he felt led to give this to me. "This" was a wad of cash he had transferred to my hand.

When I counted, it was exactly 200 dollars, and once more I was completely overwhelmed—but this time by the goodness of God and the abundance of my friend. I let the tears stream down my face as I thanked him and worshipped God for the blessing. My friend was not wealthy. He was a single young man only a year or so out of college himself, but already he was living in financial abundance.

You see, when most people hear the term financial abundance they think of someone who is financially well off, who has money flowing in and out of their bank accounts for anything they want or need. This makes sense in the natural when we recall the meaning of the word abundance. Remember according to the dictionary *abundance* means "an extremely plentiful or oversufficient quantity or supply."[1] When most people are asked to give something to a charity or a need, they quickly calculate in their minds if they have enough to spare, that is if they have any abundance to offer. While I believe we should all strive to have a natural abundance of resources in our lives to share with others when asked, I believe it is even more important to learn what Godly abundance really means and what it requires from us. To do so, let's contemplate this story from scripture:

> **And Jesus sat over against the treasury, and beheld how the people cast money into the treasury: and many that were rich cast in much. And there came a certain poor widow, and she threw in two mites, which make a farthing. And he called unto him his disciples, and saith unto them, 'Verily I say unto you, *That this poor widow hath cast more in*, than all they which have cast into the treasury: For all they did cast in of their abundance; but *she of her want did cast in all that she had*, even all her living.** (Mark 12:41–44) (Emphasis mine.)

GODLY FINANCIAL ABUNDANCE

If we are going to exercise our M.I.G.H.T. to have the abundant life Jesus promises us, then even financial abundance must spring from the establishment of a proper spiritual core. Abundance in relationship to finances cannot simply mean having enough to meet someone else's need. It absolutely must come from a reliance upon God, that he is the great provider, and that he can and he will take care of both our needs and the needs of others through us.

This story shows us the widow may have been poor financially by the world's standards, but she was rich and overflowing with her trust in God. We understand that because from her want (i.e., her need to meet her own expenses), she gave to the work of God.

Remember this story took place in the Jewish temple and the treasury represented the work of the Levites, who performed God's work throughout the temple. Therefore, her giving was to God's work. She was being obedient to God moving in her life, just like my friend when he responded to the word he received to bless me.

GIVING TO THE WORK OF GOD

This does not mean that we are only to give to things relating to God, as that might not be what God is asking of you. Here's what I mean. When you look at the verses just prior to the ones of our story about this widow woman, what do you notice?

And he said unto them in his doctrine, "Beware of the scribes, which love to go in long clothing, and love salutations in the marketplaces, And the chief seats in the synagogues, and the uppermost rooms at feasts: *Which devour widows' houses,* **and for a pretence make long prayers: these shall receive greater damnation."** (Mark 12:38–40) (Emphasis mine.)

Jesus is talking about the scribes who were religious teachers. Jesus warns us about the very individuals who were doing the work of God. Why? Because they were doing some bad things. Notice one thing Jesus particularly calls out was that they were devouring widows' houses. What does that mean? Widows had needs—financial needs—since they no longer had husbands who contributed to the household. In fact, their financial need included shelter—a house. Yet these unscrupulous scoundrels persuaded widows to give to their ministries above and beyond their own needs to the point that they lost their houses because they couldn't continue to pay for them.

Am I saying all those who are doing the work of God are like these scribes? Of course not. But beware of ministers who ask for your offering when they have private jets, mansions, and fancy cars. It's better to be giving to something when God directs you than when man encourages or pressures you. To know the difference, you must know God's voice for yourself. Hence, having the right spiritual core will help you out in that area. **"My sheep hear my voice, and I know them, and they follow me."** (John 10:27)

Whenever we give, we should do it with willingness in our hearts and the attitude that once it's out of our hands, it doesn't matter what is done with it. This is genuine financial abundance. Perhaps this is also why we are encouraged with things like these in scripture:

> **Every man according as he purposeth in his heart, so let him give; not grudgingly, or of necessity: for God loveth a cheerful giver.** (2 Corinthians 9:7)

> **Give, and it shall be given unto you; good measure, pressed down, and shaken together, and running over, shall men give into your bosom. For with the same measure that ye mete withal it shall be measured to you again.** (Luke 6:38)

Now, please don't read that previous scripture and think, *Oh that's how I get abundance, by giving, then I will receive.* That, my friends, is the completely wrong attitude and that kind of giving only makes you poor. I know there are preachers out there who will say, "If you are lacking, then give to God because he will bless you and you can't out give God." These are the type of individuals Jesus warns us about who devour widows' houses.

TURNING THE TAP

The kind of giving I'm trying to describe only comes from a place of abundance, no matter if you have surplus finances or not. It's a heart abundance and a spiritual abundance that turns the tap on God supplying the right amount of finances needed. Living with the right attitude to either get to know God or to obey and please God is the only thing that enables the promise of Luke 6:38. I know some of you will be grabbing your Bibles and asking what about this scripture?

> **Bring ye all the tithes into the storehouse, that there may be meat in mine house, and *prove me now herewith*, saith the Lord of hosts, if I will not open you the windows of heaven, and pour you out a blessing, that there shall not be room enough to receive it.** (Malachi 3:10) (Emphasis mine.)

But this scripture only proves my point, because it is encouraging us to be obedient to God's commands of giving to support his work throughout the earth.

On a side note, some will say the storehouse represents the church and that would be generally correct. To truly understand what is represented, we must understand the purpose of a storehouse. A storehouse is used for storing excess goods—well, duh you may say—but stick with me a bit. In biblical days, most people were farmers and so most storehouses were used for the storage of their crops, grain, or seed. These stored crops and grain allowed the family to continue to eat when there were no crops currently being harvested and the seed allowed them to plant new crops in the spring. Hence, the storehouse represents the place where one's resources are used to feed them and to help them multiply. This is why I say the storehouse could represent the church you attend. If your church is actively feeding you the word of God and you are growing spiritually, then by all means support your church with your tithe (a tithe represents 10 percent of your increase). However, if your church is not actively feeding you the word of God and you're able to grow through some other ministry, then…you get the point.

PUTTING IT TO THE TEST

When God says in Malachi 3:10, **"and prove me,"** he's prompting us to get to know him better because he is trustworthy and faithful. I learned this myself because I did put this promise to the test.

When I was a young Christian trying to understand tithing, I came across this scripture. Since it said I could test God to validate that I could trust him to be my provider, I thought I would. I was about to get married, we were paying for a lot of wedding expenses, setting up an apartment, paying off school loans, making car payments, and I did not have a lot of extra cash to start giving ten percent of what I was making. Still, my heart wanted to know God and if he said this was something he wanted me to be doing, I had to know it was him and not man pushing me to do it. So, I prayed and then wrote out my first tithe check. I held the check up to God (as though he couldn't see it already) and said, "God I'm doing this to prove you and to build my trust in you. If you will honor your word and send me a blessing to confirm you are in this and this is what you want from me, even though it seems I can't afford it, I will tithe as you ask." That Sunday I gave my check at church.

Later that week I received a letter from my grandmother, which was unusual as it wasn't my birthday, and we didn't write regularly. When I opened the letter, inside was a check addressed to me for 1,000 dollars! I know a thousand dollars isn't a *huge* sum of money, but it was about ten times the amount of my tithe check and totally unexpected. The most I had ever received from my grandmother previously was on certain special occasions, like my birthday or Christmas, and was only twenty dollars. I knew immediately it was God's response to my testing him. Although the letter had no mention of God in it, I knew it was God through and through. Out of all my grandparents, and relatives, she was the person who I felt was the closest to God. I called her and asked why she sent the check, since there was no mention of why in the letter. When I asked her, all she said was that she wanted to "bless her grandchildren." Of course, I thanked her profusely but when I hung up the phone, I thanked God as well. I have never looked back and continue to tithe because God honored his promise and helped me understand and trust him in that moment. He has been faithful since then providing for my every need, many times before I even knew I had one. (And yes, I tithe even when things are tight because God has proven that he can provide for all my needs.)

You will never have enough finances without the proper connection and relationship with God. It will be like chasing the wind. God's economy works differently than the world's. The world says gather until you have a surplus and then you can help others, but God says, give it away and it will come back to you. **"Cast thy bread upon the waters: for thou shalt find it after many days."** (Ecclesiastes 11:1)

Casting bread upon water may seem a little silly and that's the point. Because when you do that, the bread gets soggy and sinks, right? But God chooses words with purpose and this verse says bread is our need—we need bread to live, to get by. Casting it means you hold it loosely—you're willing to give it away without any cares. "Upon the waters" may not make sense to you, but waters flow and nurture (also biblically waters can represent peoples). In other words, when you give willingly without a care for what you will get in return or when, the work of God can flow to those who need it. At some point (after many days) your needs will be met, too, through someone else's generosity and abundance.

PRACTICAL MEASURES

Let's talk a little worldly practicality. After all, there are some basic premises even the world considers to obtain financial abundance. These are also mentioned and encouraged throughout scripture but for the sake of space, I won't provide the references here. You can do some digging on your own and I'm sure you will discover these golden nuggets of wisdom for yourself.

The first is don't spend more than you make—period! If you are living paycheck to paycheck with nothing to show for it, then something is wrong. You either need to reduce your spending or increase your paycheck. For most of us, reducing our spending is a little easier to do because we can forgo the expensive Starbucks coffee and make our own, or we can cancel the Netflix subscription and pick up a book or play games together instead. Sacrifices can be easily made with a proper reward in mind, like seeing our relationships, minds, and bank accounts grow.

Second, get out of debt and stop throwing your money away on interest because you're giving your abundance away to someone else. If you bought into the lie that interest is a good thing because of its tax deductibility, then I want you to pause and think for a moment who told you that and how much tax have you really saved? If you spent one-hundred dollars in interest to save 30 percent in taxes that means you only saved thirty dollars in taxes, and you still paid someone else seventy dollars for the privilege to do so. On the other hand, if you had paid no interest and instead paid taxes on that hundred dollars, you'd still have seventy dollars to spend any way you wanted. Better yet you could have saved seventy dollars and let it earn compounded interest on your behalf instead. Interest paid to someone else is a losing deal—*always*!

If you are in debt, then get out of debt. Start by paying off your smallest debt (by total dollar amount owed) first, and then use those payments you were making to start paying off the next smallest debt you have. Continue to repeat this process until all your debt is paid. You've got to start somewhere and with this process you will see results quicker than trying to shotgun your debts with paying a little here and a little there. When you begin to see results, you are motivated to continue, and it energizes you to believe you can do more.

In the meantime, establish a minimal emergency fund of approximately 1,000 dollars. There will be emergencies because life happens, but if you have a little money set aside it won't devastate you. If you can create this emergency fund while you're paying off your debt, all the better. Once your debt is paid off, then expand your emergency fund to equal about three to six months of your living expenses.

Once that is accomplished begin saving for your children's future education (i.e., college, tech school, vocational training, etc.). Then begin saving for retirement with as much gusto as you can. At a minimum you should shoot to save about ten to fifteen percent of your income. If you can manage it, save for your children's education and your retirement at the same time, since it is the best approach to give your retirement funds time to compound and work for you.

Look to reduce your expenses everywhere and every time you can, within reason. I say within reason because you don't want to become a miser and clamp down so hard you forget to enjoy life along the way. That only leads to envy, greed, frustration, or other unpleasant feelings. Quotes should be obtained for routine purchases like home or auto insurance at least every other year. Think twice before you purchase and shop around to ensure you are getting the best price possible to save whenever you can. Be sure to ask for discounts and extras. I do this every time I have my cars serviced and it has become so common place that the service center tells me up front they will be applying my 10 percent discount even before I ask—because they know I will.

THE ENTIRE REASON

You must look at money differently, as a tool like a screwdriver or hammer. Your job now is to save and create an abundance so God can do something through you to bless others. Blessing others is the key, and the entire reason God allows abundance to flow in our lives. Our finances should be thought of as a pipeline or conduit to allow the heavenly to flow to the earthly. God's economy revolves around giving not spending.

Realize Jesus talked at length about money in the Gospels and you can learn a lot about how to handle money, rather than having money handle you, by reading what he had to say. Scripturally we are encouraged to view money as an instrument for the accomplishment of God's purposes. We should avoid the love of money at all costs. ***"For the love of money is the root of all evil***: which while some coveted after, they have erred from the faith, and pierced themselves through with many sorrows."** (1 Timothy 6:10) (Emphasis mine.) People often misquote this scripture by saying money is the root of all evil. However, that is incorrect. It's the love of money that is the root of all evil. Money is non-emotional, it simply takes on the emotions and motives of the one who handles it. Therefore, whatever resides in your heart will be magnified and manifested through the flow of money. Will you see money as something to obtain and control, or will you relax and allow God to let it flow as needed to you and through you to others?

God calls us to simply be stewards over what he allows to flow through our lives. The word "steward" in Greek is *oikonomos* (pronounced oy-kon-om'-os) and means "steward, chamberlain (an officer who manages the household of a monarch or noble), or governor."[2] Many see stewardship as simply being a manger over the finances with which God blesses us. However, when God uses this word "steward" he is implying more than finances. He is indicating every blessing that comes into our lives, financial or otherwise, we are to oversee carefully for the benefit of God's purposes and use. You are to be the governor over the state of you. The key requirement for this is faith—believing that God allows the resource, situation, person, or whatever into our lives for his purposes to bring glory to himself and to draw us into a closer relationship with him. **"Moreover it is required in stewards, that a man be found faithful."** (1 Corinthians 4:2)

So, whether you have a lot or a little in this world, please remember that we are to pursue an eternal reward or a heavenly mansion, not an earthly one. **"Lay not up for yourselves treasures upon earth, where moth and rust doth corrupt, and where thieves break through and steal: But lay up for yourselves treasures in heaven, where neither moth nor rust doth corrupt, and where thieves do not break through nor steal: For where your treasure is, there will your heart be also."** (Matthew 6:19–21)

TAKE AWAYS

- From God's point of view, financial abundance is not defined by someone who is well off in this world, but rather who is willing to give even what little they have for the purposes of God to be fulfilled.

- Financial abundance can only flow from the correct establishment of a spiritual core, otherwise it's not about abundance, but rather about selfishness and greed.

- We must use wisdom when we are prompted to give to the work of God including our churches and other ministries. The questions we must ask ourselves are: Have we or others grown or matured spiritually because of this ministry? Is the work they are doing glorifying God? Are those who don't know God being helped and learning about God? If we are confident in the answers to those questions, then we can also be confident in our giving.

- When we decide to give, we should do it cheerfully, not out of obligation, otherwise we may as well keep it for ourselves. However, once the decision is made, we must not look back because when it's out of our hands, it belongs to the recipient and it's up to them to utilize the resources correctly. We have done our part to be generous with no strings attached.

- When it comes to giving to God's work, God encourages us to prove him—to validate that it is his will for us to be generous. This can only be done with pure motives and follow through on our part because once he proves it to us, we no longer need to test him.

- You will never have enough finances without the proper connection and relationship with God because God's economy works differently than the world's. The world's economy is based on spending, while God's is established on giving.

- There are practical steps you can take to help influence financial abundance in your life like not spending more than you make, getting out and staying out of debt, reducing your spending, and saving instead. However, we must do all of this with the proper why in mind—to allow God to build abundance in our lives to bless others and glorify him in the process.

- Money is only a tool to accomplish the purposes of God in this world. Our love should be placed in God and not in money. We are simply stewards or overseers of the blessings God allows in our lives. We need to handle them with care and with prayer.

NEXT STEPS

Sit back for a moment and reflect on your finances. Are you bogged down by debt? Is interest eating you alive? Are you existing paycheck to paycheck without an emergency fund or any savings? Do you wish that you could help others or give more to your favorite ministries? If so, ask yourself how you have been honoring God with your finances? Have you committed your finances to his purposes in your life? Are you being a good governor over the state of you? Has your stewardship over God's blessings in your life (both financial and non-financial) been admirable? If your assessment is less than pleasing, be encouraged because you too can change!

I was once in bad shape financially because I didn't realize the importance of allowing God control over all aspects of my financial life. Once, I realized God's principles over money and the importance of having a giving heart, he turned my situation around. I believe he can do it for you as well. Take your financial woes, needs, and even blessings to God in prayer. Thank him for all he has done already, all that he is doing currently, and for all that he can do in the future. Go ahead and prove him by giving as he directs you and letting him show you his capabilities. I trust that God will never let you down.

TRANSITION

We made it! We've discussed each component of our mnemonic M.I.G.H.T. (mental, interactions, God, health, and treasury) and how they relate to abundance in our lives from God's point of view. Now it's time to see how they relate to one another to help make our lives full. Join me in the next chapter and see how it's all connected.

13
IT'S ALL CONNECTED

*"Life in abundance comes
only through great love."*
–Elbert Hubbard

WE'VE PROGRESSED THROUGH OUR analogy of the abundance wheel and each of life's spokes and identified the spiritual hub we can trust to transport us to the place of abundant living. Hopefully we have gained some insight as to what true abundance from God's perspective means in each area of our lives, that is mentally and emotionally, relationally and socially, spiritually, physically, and financially. Perhaps you've come to realize that true abundance isn't always what it appears to be on the surface and sometimes it takes more consideration and thought to be able to recognize it.

What I hope to help you see now is that each of these areas of our lives is fully impacted by the others, especially at the place the spokes meet the hub. To put it another way, as we focus to develop our spiritual core and allow it to influence us, it will have an overwhelming impact on the other areas of our lives. The first ten verses of Proverbs three clearly shows us these relationships.

My son, forget not my law; but let thine heart keep my commandments: For length of days, and long life, and peace, shall they add to thee. Let not mercy and

truth forsake thee: bind them about thy neck; write them upon the table of thine heart: So shalt thou find favour and good understanding in the sight of God and man. (Proverbs 3:1–4)

In the very first two sentences we are encouraged to keep God's commandments because they will provide us a long life and peace. Hence the spiritual core (following God's commandments) impacts both the health or physical spoke (long life) and the mental or emotional spoke (peace). Continuing to the second two sentences we see that if we follow mercy and truth that we will obtain favor from God and man. Therefore, we understand the spiritual core also impacts our relationships (God and interactions spokes).

Trust in the Lord with all thine heart; and lean not unto thine own understanding. In all thy ways acknowledge him, and he shall direct thy paths. Be not wise in thine own eyes: fear the Lord, and depart from evil. It shall be health to thy navel, and marrow to thy bones. (Proverbs 3:5–8)

Here we see that when we trust in God, he directs our path, which represents our decision making—our mental spoke. We realize that by following God, it offers us health and strength. So once again we see the spiritual core's influence on our physical spoke.

Honour the Lord with thy substance, and with the firstfruits of all thine increase: So shall thy barns be filled with plenty, and thy presses shall burst out with new wine. (Proverbs 3:9-10)

Hence, we conclude that maintaining our spiritual core will also cause our financial spoke to flourish. Since all these areas are interconnected and each impacts the other, we must seek balance throughout our lives. We don't want one area to be stronger than the others because the ride down life's road will end up bumpy or wobbly. When we come up short in one area, an abundance in another area can help make up the difference for a while, but if left that way both areas will eventually become drained. Understanding the connections to our spiritual core can help us with balance to recognize our short falls and make corrections quickly.

IS GOD TRYING TO GET YOUR ATTENTION?

Any way we turn, we are impacted by what is happening in our spiritual core in the other areas of our lives. It can be hard to realize an obstacle in one area may be a result of neglecting our spiritual core, especially during difficult times. In fact, God may even allow one area of our life to suffer to get us to refocus on him and restrengthen our core. Please don't misunderstand me and think every difficulty and challenge we have in life is a result of God trying to get our attention. We must realize life truly is a complicated mess and it's just a part of being alive to have and face challenges. However, it's what we do and what we learn because of those challenges that matters most.

Just like with physical exercise, our body benefits most when we focus on exercising our core. By improving our core physically, we gain strength and stability in the other areas of our physical being. It's not easy to do unending crunches and ab workouts, because we get tired quickly and it hurts, but it's the exercise and pain that allows for great gains to be made (the loss of excess weight, strength developed, balance obtained, etc.).

If we realize that scripture tells us, **"For whom the Lord loveth he chasteneth, and scourgeth every son whom he** receiveth" (Hebrews 12:6), and **"As many as I love, I rebuke and chasten: be zealous therefore, and repent"** (Revelation 3:19) then we should also realize that although it can be painful, it's not meant to discourage us.

At the beginning of each of these scriptural statements from God, it clearly tells us that he allows the chastisement, scourging, and rebuke because he loves us. He is an amazing Father in that way. After all, if he didn't love us, he wouldn't bother with us. Yet, it's because of his great love for us that he wants the best for us. He wants us to have abundance in every area of our lives, and so he disciplines us to keep us going in the right direction and to keep improving.

PROSPERING FOR GOD

We are encouraged in John 15:5 with these words, **"I am the vine, ye are the branches: He that abideth in me, and I in him, the same bringeth forth much fruit: for without me ye can do nothing."**

Why does it matter to God that we "bring forth much fruit" or in other words have abundance? The answer is found a few verses later in John 15:8, **"Herein is my Father glorified, that ye bear much fruit; so shall ye be my disciples."**

The fruit we bear or the abundance we share is so that God is glorified. And how is God glorified? When we share him and his blessings with others because it helps them see where and how the blessings were obtained. They, too, can turn to God, thereby experiencing him and his blessings for themselves. Hence, abundance in our lives should allow for others to experience abundance in their own lives as well.

So, please do not be discouraged by the statement of John 15:2, **"Every branch in me that beareth not fruit he taketh away: and every branch that beareth fruit, he purgeth it, that it may bring forth more fruit."** This is what I was trying to say earlier. God allows us to suffer or be purged in some areas of our lives so that we will refocus on him and regain our perspective on the reason for his blessings and abundance in our lives—that we may not lose out on the joy of sharing it with others.

Here's a little clue I found in that scripture for you, and this is also a reason I really enjoy the King James version of the Bible. As I pointed out earlier, the little "th" on the end of the words implies the meaning of continuance. So, when you read a word like purgeth it means continuously purges. In every-day English we would say purges or purged, but that would imply a one-time event. Referencing purgeth, we would say he purges and keeps on purging. In other words, God keeps his eye on us all the time to ensure we are continually growing and developing, so he's going to correct our course whenever we need it. Thank God for that!

A COURSE CORRECTION

If you are reading this and realizing God is currently doing some purging in your life, you're experiencing that course correction. What do you need to do to help the process rather than resisting it? To find the answer, we must understand the reason God allows these things to happen, so we refer to Revelation 3:19 which tells us God loves and corrects us so that we will "repent" (or course correct).

What does it mean to course correct? It simply means to alter a course to get back on track. Maybe we were heading down the right road or path, but something distracted us and we got sidetracked or onto another track other than the original one. To get back on the right track, the first step is to recognize and admit it. The next step is to turn around and get back on the correct track we once were on and continue forward. Sometimes this takes a while and can be painful, but there is a sense of relief when we know we are back on the right road.

For example, I used to have an hour-long commute home from downtown Milwaukee. There were times I worked long hours, even twelve- to fourteen-hour days and then had to head home. Once after a night of not sleeping well and working a very long day, I was very tired and not paying attention. I missed my exit. The next exit was eight miles down the highway, and it meant not only did I have to travel that far to exit, but then I'd have to turn around and go back the eight miles to the correct exit. It was not fun, and I learned quickly I needed to pay closer attention—even more so when I knew I was tired so I wouldn't have to endure that again.

Repentance is not only acknowledging when we messed up but recognizing that we will have to suffer the resulting consequences. In the end things can get worked out and be better. Let's not fool ourselves—we're human after all, and we all make mistakes. Scripture tells, **"For all have sinned, and come short of the glory of God."** (Romans 3:23) There are times we are going to be a little tired and not paying as close attention as we should, but that's all right. God understands, and he gives us opportunities to get it right through course corrections.

If we confess our sins, he is faithful and just to forgive us our sins, and to cleanse us from all unrighteousness. (1 John 1:9)

DOING EVEN BETTER

However, we must realize that God's purging isn't just because we made a mistake, sometimes it's because we are doing right! Yes, that's correct—sometimes things are going well and suddenly you are experiencing a purging in your life because God knows you can be doing even better. Reread John 15:2—the branch is already bearing fruit (it's doing well), but God purges it anyway so it can bear more fruit (it can do even better).

Think of it this way. Your life is like gold dug out of the raw earth. There's value simply because the piece of earth contains the gold within it, but it's mixed in with other elements (e.g., clay, granite, etc.). If you take that hunk of gold and put it in the fire, then you can purify the gold and it becomes even more valuable because it's no longer bound to the other elements. Perhaps that's why 1 Peter 4:12–13 says, **"Beloved, think it not strange concerning the fiery trial which is to try you, as though some strange thing happened unto you: But rejoice, inasmuch as ye are partakers of Christ's sufferings; that, when his glory shall be revealed, ye may be glad also with exceeding joy."** And 1 Peter 1:7 says, **"That the trial of your faith, being much more precious than of gold that perisheth, though it be tried with fire, might be found unto praise and honour and glory at the appearing of Jesus Christ."**

These scriptures should be a relief to us because we know that whatever God allows in our lives is always for our benefit—to help us grow and experience true abundance.

According to 2 Corinthians 8:2 which says, **"How that in a great trial of affliction the abundance of their joy and their deep poverty abounded unto the riches of their liberality,"** trials and affliction can cause us to focus on the true source of joy, which is God and his provision through it all. So, although one may be considered materially impoverished, they can still possess great riches because of their kindness.

If we can grasp the concepts God is trying to show us in his word and through the things he allows us to experience in our lives, then we can truly have abundance in him, which flows through us outward toward others. Jesus said, **"For whosoever hath, to him shall be given, and he shall have more *abundance*: but whosoever hath not, from him shall be taken away even that he hath."** (Matthew 13:12) (Emphasis mine.) I believe he was telling us that if we accept his word and live by the truth of what real abundance is—even if we start with what seems to be little—and we act upon that knowledge and exercise our M.I.G.H.T., the little we have will grow into greater abundance. However, on the other hand, if we ignore, brush off, or even reject the truth of God's word, then the little we have will be lost, and we will be found empty in the difficult times and left with nothing meaningful or lasting.

THE CONNECTING POINT

Jesus came that we might have life and that we might have it more abundantly and we have seen that he came to free us from sin and the result of sin, which is death. **"For the wages of sin is death; but the gift of God is eternal life through Jesus Christ our Lord."** (Romans 6:23) However, Romans 5:17 tells us, **"For if by one man's offence death reigned by one; much more they which receive abundance of grace and of the gift of righteousness shall reign in life by one, Jesus Christ."** This tells us because of Adam's sin in the Garden of Eden, we have all been affected by sin and its resulting consequence of death. Jesus paid the price for us and provided grace through repentance, which if we accept, we shall have its resulting consequence and reign in life (or experience the abundant life he promises).

One last thought I'd like to share here is something I found in 1 Chronicles 29:2 **"Now *I have prepared* with all my might *for the house of my God* the gold for things to be made of gold, and the silver for things of silver, and the brass for things of brass, the iron for things of iron, and wood for things of wood; onyx stones, and stones to be set, glistering stones, and of divers colours, and all manner of precious stones, and marble stones in abundance."** (Emphasis mine.)

This is a quote from King David, who desired to build God a permanent temple rather than a roaming tent, and so he labored during his life to accumulate the things it would take to build the temple and make it splendid, which he referred to as the "house of my God." We are told of the many things he gathered and stored up in preparation. In fact, there are several scriptures that also indicate the abundances he had could not be measured or weighed because they were so numerous.

Why was it important to David to build God a grand temple? Because he knew the importance of drawing others to God. Others would hear of this amazing building, want to see it for themselves, and by coming into this temple they would get the chance to interact with and experience David's amazing God for themselves. It was a way to honor God and thank him for all the blessings he bestowed on David, but it was also a way to invite others to know God.

Understand David's preparation took years. He gathered a little here in this victory, a little more with that victory, and he kept doing so until he finally had an abundance. He stopped counting what he had and simply trusted it was enough for God's purposes.

I want us to also understand this scripture tells us that we have become the temple of God because of Jesus's sacrifice on our behalf.

Know ye not that ye are the temple of God, and that the Spirit of God dwelleth in you? (1 Corinthians 3:16)

What? know ye not that your body is the temple of the Holy Ghost which is in you, which ye have of God, and ye are not your own? (1 Corinthians 6:19)

If we look at David's statement as our own, we can see whatever God allows in our lives through his abundance is to be used to build his house—where he resides—and share with others so they too can witness the grace and blessings of God and potentially experience him for themselves. This is why I stress that the connecting point for abundance in every area of our lives must come from the proper spiritual core, where we commit ourselves fully to God, and in turn his abundance flows through us to benefit not only our lives but the lives of those around us.

Like David, it's not going to happen overnight for you either. There will be trials, temptations, difficulties, and challenges that you will have to overcome to stay focused and on course. You must pay attention even when you are tired and weary, but you can trust that God will assist you to stay on the right path. In the meantime, you can prepare by reading his word, following his commands, and storing up knowledge, understanding, and wisdom from the victories you experience in your own life. Then you can relax and simply trust that there will always be enough for God's purposes in your life. Now that truly is abundant living!

TAKE AWAYS

- Abundance from God's perspective isn't always as it appears on the surface and sometimes it takes more consideration and thought to be able to recognize it.

- As we focus to develop our spiritual core and allow it to influence us, it will have an overwhelming impact in the other areas of our lives.

- God allows difficulties in our lives to help provide us with course corrections. Through the hardships we endure, we can see the weak areas of our lives that need strengthening. It's a form of God's mercy to allow these things to help get us back on track, rather than letting us continue down a road of self-destruction.

- God wants us to prosper but not stagnate in that prosperity. Therefore, he is constantly purging us of things that keep us from being all he intends for us. This purging can seem difficult but if faced with a positive attitude, we can keep from prolonging the process and see prosperity sooner in the areas that have been purged.

- God's abundance will not be experienced overnight in any area of our lives. Instead, it will be developed a little at a time as we learn and grow, especially as we gain victories over the challenges we face—specifically those that may push us to distrust God and his promises.

NEXT STEPS

When you consider your life are there areas that seem to be out of balance compared to the rest? Are the difficulties in this area of your life seeming to repeat themselves? In other words, are you going through a cyclical pattern? If so, perhaps God is providing you with a course correction in this area of your life. Think honestly about the situation and see if there is some violation being made against God's word or his commands. This might be an area where you need to repent and commit to following God rather than your own will.

Have you committed to allowing God to be the center of your life, your spiritual core, so that the other areas of your life can benefit from the connecting impact? If you want abundance in every area of your life according to God's perspective, are you willing to seek his purposes rather than yours? If so, spend some time in prayer and let him know that. Ask him to guide you through his word to gain a deeper understanding of what pleases him. Search scripture and learn more about this amazing God who loves you and wants you to prosper with abundance.

TRANSITION

We have gained so much through our journey of abundance together. It would be a shame if the knowledge and understanding we have gained was stolen from us. Therefore, we must learn how to prevent the thief of abundant living from doing us any harm. Continue with me into the next chapter to see how we can deter this persistent menace.

14
DETERRING THE THIEF

*"The thief you must fear the most is
not the one who steals mere things."*
–ANN-MARIE MACDONALD

IT WAS LATE AT night, and we had been driving over eight hours to get home. It was snowing, cold, and dark and we were all extremely tired. The week before was very relaxing, filled with warmth and excitement, since we celebrated Christmas with my grandparents in northern Wisconsin on the edge of Lake Superior. We did some great sledding down a very steep and long hill that led from my grandparents' house down to the beach. We shoveled off a patch of snow-covered ice on the lake's edge to do some ice skating. We drank hot chocolate and ate delicious meals and sweet treats. And we unwrapped loads of presents, played numerous games together, and laughed hard at various stories and jokes told. It was a great week, and although it was tough to say good-bye, we loaded up our small car with all our luggage and new goodies and made the long trek home.

After the long drive and being cramped in the back seat with all the things we were taking home with us, my legs were stiff, my back was sore, and I was sleepy. As a typical cranky thirteen-year-old, to say I was looking forward to getting home was an understatement. I breathed a sigh of relief when we pulled into the driveway and my dad got out to open the garage door (in those days most people had to manually unlock and lift the garage door to enter). We pulled the car into the garage and began gathering some things to take inside with us as we lumbered out of the car. When we entered our house, we were not hit with the expected welcoming warm air of home but rather the air was just as cold as it was outside. We turned on the lights and noticed the disaster that lay before us. Things were strewn on the floor as if a tornado had ripped through the house, but the house structure was unaffected and still standing.

We quickly walked through the house and the entirety of it was the same—everything was turned upside down. Drawers were pulled out, emptied, and thrown to the floor; closets were also emptied with the belongings tossed on the floor—the place was in complete shambles. My dad quickly called the police and we waited. While waiting, my dad discovered a large picture window in the back of the house was smashed as the point of entry and the reason for the cold within the house. We had been robbed.

A tremendous feeling of violation and disturbance filled us. We discovered the thief or thieves had stolen a few relatively immaterial things—a camera, some cash, and some other small items. It seemed their real intent was to cause destruction and upheaval. Unfortunately, the police never found the responsible party or parties. Therefore, it took a long time to feel safe again in our own home. Shortly after that my parents installed a security system in our home to help provide a better sense of peace.

ADDRESSING THE THIEF

We all experience dramatic shifts in our lives. One moment we are in a good place where everything seems to be fine and then the next—*BAM*—something knocks us down and we don't even know why. We're left reeling, looking for answers, and trying to recoup. It's hard and it's painful. We must do our best to watch for and fend off the things that try to steal our joy. We must fight against the thief of abundance.

Since we're reaching the end of our journey together, I would be remiss if I didn't provide some instruction on the very first part of our main scripture text. Let's refresh ourselves with our main scripture reference once more, **"The thief cometh not, but for to steal, and to kill, and to destroy: I am come that they might have life, and that they might have it more abundantly."** (John 10:10)

We've focused on the reason Jesus came—to give us the opportunity for life. We've described what life means and what abundant life is. As a part of our discussion, we've also indicated that we must work at obtaining the abundant life promised to us by exercising our M.I.G.H.T. But, up to this point we haven't talked much about the thief. He is waiting to strike and upset our abundance at any moment.

First, we must again identify the thief. Who is he? In chapter two we identified the thief as Satan. He's the serpent in the Garden of Eden who stole the life right out of Adam and Eve, and he's still slithering around today to steal our abundance, kill our dreams, and destroy our lives. Just ignoring the thief is not enough. We are warned in scripture, **"Be sober, be vigilant; because your adversary the devil, as a roaring lion, walketh about, seeking whom he may devour."** (1 Peter 5:8)

WATCH AND WATCH SOME MORE

The best deterrent in keeping the thief at bay is as Peter says, having a good offense. We are told to be "sober," which is the Greek word *nēphō* (pronounced nay'-fo) and not only means "to be sober (abstain from wine)," but "to watch, be calm and collected in spirit, to be temperate, dispassionate and circumspect."[1] Examine the next word Peter used, "vigilant," which is the Greek word *grēgoreō* (pronounced gray-gor-yoo'-o) and means "to watch, to keep awake, give strict attention to, be cautious and active."[2] When you combine these two words, they seem a little redundant because they both include this idea of watching. In essence you could say he's telling us to watch and watch some more. That's how important it is that we do so. It's so important that it's worth repeating.

However, it's more than that. Peter is communicating the image of a soldier on watch. A soldier when on duty is responsible to be sober, awake while others rest, calm if the enemy approaches, cautious in his duties, and sound the alarm when necessary. That's how we are to be over the abundance in our lives. We are soldiers in a war against the devil whose goal is to defeat us.

Satan is described as a "roaring lion, walking about, seeking whom he may devour." A hungry lion paces back and forth looking for the weak ones in a pack. He doesn't have much energy to exude because of his hunger. So, he roars to frighten them, in hopes they will freeze in their tracks allowing the lion to catch them without much effort on the lion's part.

As soldiers in this war against the devil, we are encouraged by several passages of scripture:

> **For though we walk in the flesh, we do not war after the flesh: (for the weapons of our warfare are not carnal, but mighty through God to the pulling down of strong holds;) casting down imaginations, and every high thing that exalteth itself against the knowledge**

of God, and bringing into captivity every thought to the obedience of Christ. (2 Corinthians 10:3–5)

For we wrestle not against flesh and blood, but against principalities, against powers, against the rulers of the darkness of this world, against spiritual wickedness in high places. (Ephesians 6:12)

We must realize that our fight is not in this flesh, rather it's a spiritual battle. When negativity and oppressive thoughts come against us, we must stop and realize they may not be derived from the situation in which we find ourselves, but rather they might just be a spiritual attack coming from the enemy to distract us. This is why it is so important to have the right spiritual core. By doing so we will know how to fight this spiritual battle and come out victorious in the end.

YOU AND GOD

Are we really expected to fight the spiritual battle? Yes, otherwise we wouldn't have been told we have "weapons" in 2 Corinthians 10:3–5. In fact, isn't it interesting that our weapons are called "mighty," or could I say M.I.G.H.T.Y.? Since you're allowing it, then you probably want to know what the "Y" stands for in M.I.G.H.T.Y. That's a simple one—it's You!

You already know that to obtain abundance in your life, it takes exercising your M.I.G.H.T. However, to maintain abundance and keep the thief at bay, it also takes you and your effort. You are the one encouraged to pull down strongholds. What are those strongholds? They are places and ways of thinking in your mind. How do we know this? Because the next phrase tells us that to pull them (the strongholds) down you must cast down imaginations (the things you think) and bring your thoughts into captivity. Into captivity of what, or better yet to whom? Jesus Christ! When we obey God and his word, we gain the power to recognize our faulting thinking and the lies the enemy tries to get us to believe. By recognizing them, we can refuse and reject them.

We understand now why scripture informs us, **"Lest Satan should get an advantage of us: for we are not ignorant of his devices."** (2 Corinthians 2:11) We indeed are not ignorant that the devil lies to us and now we know what to do about it. This is how we resist the devil—by refusing to accept his fear and lies. **"Submit yourselves therefore to God. Resist the devil, and he will flee from you."** (James 4:7) Notice here the prerequisite is that we must submit ourselves to God, that is follow his instructions. Another way of looking at this is that *it's going to take you and God working together* to overcome the enemy. You cannot do it alone—we all need God's help.

I want to share something interesting related to how the enemy tries to keep us from working together with God and it has to do with the number thirteen. The number has a negative connotation to it. We must ask ourselves why? People are convinced it's an evil number and so they associate it with the devil. How did that come about? Perhaps it was simply good propaganda by the devil himself to defile the number.

The essence of the number is made up of two numbers added together: six and seven equals thirteen. The number six in scripture represents man since he was created on the sixth day of creation. The number seven in scripture represents spiritual completeness or perfection and often is referred to as God's number since God is the only one who is spiritually perfect. When you combine six with seven to equal thirteen some claim it represents man trying to put himself in the place of God. That is definitely a bad thing and it's the thing the devil tried to do himself because of his pride and so he fell from heaven. However, the main emphasis of scripture teaches us that we should strive to be more like God and his character. If that is true, then the better interpretation of the number is simply man and God working together to make man more spiritually complete.

The enemy has taken a perfectly good number and corrupted it in most people's minds. That's what he does—attempts to keep man and God apart—and he's good at it. He's good at being a devil. But we are not to be "ignorant of his devices" (his methods) so we need to be awake, alert and strive to reject even these small maneuvers of his to make us think incorrectly, accept fear, or believe a lie.

THE THIEF MUST PAY

We must take measures to keep the thief at bay and prevent him from taking our abundance. We also want him to return what was stolen *and* pay the redemption price. What do I mean by this?

In the Old Testament we are told if a thief took something and they were caught with it, they were required to restore the original and then some to make the party they stole from whole.

> **If a man shall steal an ox, or a sheep, and kill it, or sell it; he shall restore five oxen for an ox, and four sheep for a sheep. If a thief be found breaking up, and be smitten that he die, there shall no blood be shed for him. If the sun be risen upon him, there shall be blood shed for him; for he should make full restitu-**

tion; if he have nothing, then he shall be sold for his theft. If the theft be certainly found in his hand alive, whether it be ox, or ass, or sheep; he shall restore double. (Exodus 22:1–4)

We see by this that our steps are to repent, follow God with all our M.I.G.H.T., stay vigilant about spiritual things, and watch out for the enemy's lies. If he steals our abundance, when we recognize it and trust in God to work with us, all should be restored and then some.

One last thing to mention as we fight the spiritual battles that come our way (we don't go looking for them directly but fight them when we encounter them), we need to be properly equipped. There is a lot to say on this subject, and there are better books out there than this one to address the topic of spiritual warfare. Nonetheless, when a soldier goes out to fight, he needs to be properly outfitted. We are told in scripture:

Wherefore take unto you the whole armour of God, that ye may be able to withstand in the evil day, and having done all, to stand. Stand therefore, having your loins girt about with truth, and having on the breastplate of righteousness; and your feet shod with the preparation of the gospel of peace; above all, taking the shield of faith, wherewith ye shall be able to quench all the fiery darts of the wicked. And take the helmet of salvation, and the sword of the Spirit, which is the word of God: praying always with all prayer and supplication in the Spirit, and watching thereunto with all perseverance and supplication for all saints. (Ephesians 6:13–18)

There are a few things to note here. First, realize this is all commentary regarding the spiritual, not the physical. Paul is not telling us to walk around in physical armor every day. Rather, he is saying we need to be honest in the most intimate places of ourselves like our hearts and minds (represented by the loins), so we can be aware and focused on truth even when dealing with ourselves.

We need our hearts protected by God's righteousness (the breastplate) because it is God who can nourish our hearts and our desires. Wherever we go we need to take the gospel with us and allow it to work its peace in our lives and in the lives of those around us (having our feet shod, or permanently affixed, to the purpose of the gospel, i.e., the spreading of the good news). And, when we are attacked by fiery darts (trials and difficulties thrown at us by the enemy), if we have faith (our shield) that God is working with us to protect us, guide us, and help us be the best that we can be, then those darts will fizzle out without even a trace of smoke left upon us. Having the helmet of salvation upon us means our minds should be focused on what God has provided for us through his great sacrifice—our salvation. Let us never forget this!

Lastly, when we do need to attack the enemy head on, we need a good grip and an understanding of God's word to do so—it is our sword. When used properly, it will flush out our motives and the motives of those around us.

For the word of God is quick, and powerful, and sharper than any two-edged sword, piercing even to the dividing asunder of soul and spirit, and of the joints and marrow, and is a discerner of the thoughts and intents of the heart. (Hebrews 4:12)

I hope this encourages you to not be placid about facing the thief of our abundance, but instead it prompts you to be awake, alert, and on guard to protect and maintain the abundance God allows you to experience in your life.

TAKE AWAYS

- We all experience dramatic shifts in our lives that can knock us down or blindside us, so we must do our best to watch for and fight off the things that try to steal our joy.

- Our common enemy, Satan or the devil, who is the thief of abundance is also referred to as a roaring lion on the prowl, looking to take easy advantage of us. We cannot just ignore him. We must be vigilant and watch and watch some more. In other words, stand guard over the abundance God has allowed to flow through our lives.

- Our battle is not against others in the flesh, but it's a spiritual battle that typically is waged in our minds. We must examine our thoughts and determine from where the negativity and oppressive thoughts are really stemming. Most of the time it's just the enemy's ploy to distract us. Having the right spiritual core can help us know when and how to fight off these attacks.

- You cannot defeat the thief alone. You need God on your side to properly deter the enemy from your territory. The first step in resisting the devil's attacks is submission to God, his word, and his ways. It's by surrendering to God that victory over the devil flows to us since Jesus has already defeated the enemy upon the cross.

- When we recognize that the enemy has stolen some of our abundance, there is nothing wrong with praying to God that the thief be made to pay restitution. It's a scriptural principle. When we repent of our mistakes and strive to live in a way that pleases God, he will command the enemy to restore our abundance—even to levels that may exceed what we had before (see the book of Job as an example).

- Since we are in a spiritual battle, it is vital that we are properly equipped. Study Ephesians 6:13–18 to see the areas God wants to be covered when we are in sync with him. You will notice most are defensive items, meaning we don't usually set out to fight the enemy, but should the fight come to us, we can be ready and utilize God's sword (the word of God) to defeat the attack.

NEXT STEPS

Have you been blindsided by something recently? Are you struggling with situations that seem to be draining you of your abundance? Are you having difficulty putting your finger on the reason for the negativity you're facing? Perhaps you are under attack—spiritual attack. Have you considered that the enemy has singled you out, especially if you love God and are doing your best to please him? Take these things to God in prayer and ask God to reveal the ways the enemy is trying to trip you up and steal your abundance. Ask for his help. Remember if you submit to God, then you can resist the devil, and he must flee from you. So be sure—100 percent confident—you are submitted to God. Are you following his word and not your own will? Are you taking decisions to him in prayer rather than deciding and then seeking his approval?

If you are submitted, then next ask yourself if you're resisting the devil. Are you refusing to entertain the negativity? Are you calling out his lies? Resisting means you may need to institute some changes and new ways of thinking.

If you are submitting to God and resisting the devil, then lastly make sure you are properly covered according to Ephesians 6:13–18. Review the scripture and pray about any weak spots you may have. If you do, you will start to see the abundance God promises flowing through you in return. Remember to ask God to make the thief pay now that you have caught him in the act of trying to take your abundance. Ask God to help you reach new levels of abundance so you can bless and help others know more about him.

TRANSITION

I am so glad you have made it this far. You now have some tools to help you hold onto your abundance from God without letting the thief take it from you. However, sometimes, it's not so easy to recognize when we are under attack. Therefore, we need the assistance of others to help us identify our weaknesses. We all can use support from time to time to fight our battles. Let's talk about this in the next chapter and find out how we can assist each other in this journey of abundance.

15
A LITTLE HELP PLEASE

"If you want to go fast, go alone.
If you want to go far, go together."
Aғrican proverb

ONE OF MY FAVORITE scriptures is Proverbs 27:17 because it reminds me that we need each other, and it reads **"Iron sharpeneth iron; so a man sharpeneth the countenance of his friend."** The author of this proverb (perhaps King Solomon) most likely chose to use the idea of iron sharpening iron because this life is a battle. We all know it. We face challenges, difficulties, and unexpected circumstances daily. Spiritual warfare rages all around us, whether we perceive it or not.

Hence, when you grasp the picture in your mind of a soldier girded up in the armor of God and wielding the sword of the spirit (see Ephesians chapter 6), you also understand that as a sword clashes against the weapons of the enemy there will be dings, scrapes, slight gouges, and perhaps even some minor twisting of the sword's metal that occurs because of heavy fighting.

Soldiers were personally responsible to ensure their weapon was always ready for peak performance. They regularly sharpened their sword to ensure that it was ready to perform at a moment's notice—especially after a grueling battle. They wouldn't wait because they never knew when they would be called upon to fight again. It could be at any moment and going into a fight with a dull weapon could mean exerting a lot more energy than necessary or potentially death.

SHARPENING THE SWORD

Let us pause here for a moment and consider that the author of the proverb is not saying that one sword can be used to sharpen another sword—that is nearly impossible. So, what is the author of the verse conveying to us? For us to understand it, we must know the meaning of the original Hebrew word used and translated as "iron." It is the Hebrew word *barzel* (pronounced bar-zel') and means "iron, head or smith and is used throughout the Bible as iron, iron ore, tool of iron or harness, strength or oppression."[1]

We know a smith or blacksmith is one who works with metals and knows how to sharpen swords. Therefore, we can rephrase the proverb as "it takes a smith to sharpen iron." Now that makes a lot more sense, doesn't it? Someone on the same level cannot help an equal (another foot soldier) advance. It takes someone who knows a little more about the subject, who has experienced more, or practiced more to be able to boost or help the one on a lower level to come up another level. Think of it this way, if you are on level five and you want to get to level six you cannot have someone on level five help you get there since they've never experienced level six themselves and they don't know what it takes to get there. But if you find a level six person or higher to help you, chances are you'll have a much better opportunity to reach level six.

So, while this scripture reminds us we need each other, it also encourages us to find a personal coach or mentor—someone who can help us sharpen and advance to be more useful. The sharper the tool, the more precise the cut can be. You wouldn't drag your sword into the operating room to remove someone's appendix, for example. It would be cumbersome and hard to be precise with the exact cuts needing to be made. The size and width of the sword's blade would cut more of the patient than desired and cause other problems during the procedure. If you thin the blade through the process of making it sharper, eventually you'd have the thinnest cutting edge necessary to carry out the procedure without unnecessary risks.

That's the purpose of a coach and we all need one at times, especially in light of this scripture. What is the relationship between this scripture and our purpose? The author uses a transitionary word after the declaration that iron sharpens iron—the word "so." By using this word he's preparing us for the point of the phrase—man sharpening the countenance of his friend. To comprehend what this is saying to us, let us examine the word "countenance," which is the Hebrew word *pānîm* (pronounced paw-neem') and means "before, face, presence, because, sight, from, person, upon, open, toward and in front of."[2]

LIFT UP YOUR COUNTENANCE

We can see that most interpret the word countenance as a person's face. However, I believe it's more than that. I believe it means a person's outlook or even his purpose or destiny. What is a person's face, or more specifically, for what is a person's face used? Isn't it the means through which a person interacts with their surroundings? It's the place they express themselves. The place through which they communicate what's happening within them to the outside world through their smiles, frowns, shining eyes, or tears. In other words, others can influence what we are expressing to the outside world because they are affecting what's going on within us.

We've covered in previous chapters that our emotions, and resulting actions are derived out of what we think. Hence, a coach can help us transform our thinking to help solicit different emotions and resulting actions than we would have had on our own. Remember getting us to level six thinking rather than remaining on level five is the goal of a proper coach.

Let me further illustrate the point here with a story out of Luke chapter 9 specifically verses 28–30, **"And it came to pass about an eight days after these sayings, he took Peter and John and James, and went up into a mountain to pray. And as he prayed, the fashion of his countenance was altered, and his raiment was white and glistering. And, behold, there talked with him two men, which were Moses and Elias."**

Why does the story begin by pointing out a period of time, "about an eight days after?" I believe it's because the number eight represents new beginnings. For example, we know that there were eight people saved on Noah's ark when God allowed the world a new beginning (Genesis chapters 6 and 7). A Jewish baby boy was to be circumcised on the eighth day (Leviticus 12:2–3). These are just a couple of reasons I believe eight means new beginnings (not to mention that the new birth or spiritual new beginning is described in the first eight verses of John chapter three [and in which the number three represents the Spirit]). Here Jesus showed Peter, John, and James a new beginning that would take place due to the fulfillment of his purpose in their lives. His discipling (coaching) of them had and would continue to take them to new levels. Then what happened?

It says as they prayed Jesus's countenance was altered, but it wasn't just his face that was changed. Even his clothing was changed and became white and glistened. Moses and Elias (Elijah) even appeared and talked with Jesus. What did they talk about? Verse 31 tells us what they discussed, **"Who appeared in glory, and spake of his decease which he should accomplish at Jerusalem."** In other words, they discussed his future, his outlook, his potential, and his purpose. This is why I believe when you sharpen someone's "countenance," you are helping to sharpen their outlook or enabling them to fulfil their destiny or purpose.

A SPIRITUAL COACH

A good coach helps us get unstuck when we feel like we've stopped growing. They provide correct direction and see blind spots before we do so we don't hit the wall. The goal of coaching is to truly help someone see things through a different lens and empower them to reach a new level so they can fulfill their purpose here on this earth. For that type of coaching to be successful, it must be focused on the spiritual core if the goal is to reach an abundant life, which I believe should be the ultimate goal of all of us.

We know there are coaches in every area of life. There are physical fitness coaches, financial coaches, relationship counselors, mental health counselors, and so on. We may need specific coaching in one or more of these areas at times throughout our lives. In fact, I encourage it. When you feel a little stuck and you're not making progress in one of these areas, consider getting the specific help you need to get over the hump. The problem is, as we've previously discussed, these areas are only spokes within our wheel and while this type of coaching can strengthen a particular spoke, it will not address the overall need or core of our lives. That's why we also need a spiritual coach to address our spiritual core. Many will turn to their pastors to act as that spiritual coach, and while this is very beneficial, it may not be enough. Why do I say that?

Most pastors have demanding schedules and cannot spend adequate one-on-one time with an individual to properly develop them. Also, while trained in the things of the Spirit, pastors may have a very good understanding of the spiritual core but not have a good understanding of finances, for example, or another spoke of life. So, having your pastor on your coaching team is a good idea but so is having several other coaches to round out your abundant life. We are encouraged in scripture with the following verses:

> **Where no counsel is, the people fall: but in the *multitude of counsellors* there is safety.** (Proverbs 11:14) (Emphasis mine.)

> **Without counsel purposes are disappointed: but in the *multitude of counsellors* they are established.** (Proverbs 15:22) (Emphasis mine.)

We all need coaching and according to these verses, we should seek counsel in every area of our lives—not just from one individual, but rather from a multitude of counsellors. Having a multitude of counsellors allows for a safety net in our lives. The key is to ensure that every counselor we include in our lives is also centered around the same spiritual core, so that we don't end up with conflicting advice which can lead to confusion and harm. (Recall one of my other favorite scriptures informs us that God is not the author of confusion see 1 Corinthians 14:33.)

We must always evaluate the counsel we receive against something unchangeable and true before implementing it. For me and hopefully for you, it is the unalterable word of God. Every piece of advice we receive should be held up against the light of scripture to see if it is beneficial and worthwhile to apply to our lives. After all scripture instructs us:

Beloved, believe not every spirit, but try the spirits whether they are of God: because many false prophets are gone out into the world. (1 John 4:1)

DISCERNING COUNSEL

This is how we exercise *discernment*, which according to the dictionary simply means "the act or process of exhibiting keen insight and good judgment."[3] Another scripture furthers this idea by stating:

Study to shew thyself approved unto God, a workman that needeth not to be ashamed, rightly dividing the word of truth. (2 Timothy 2:15)

The word "dividing" here is the Greek word *orthotomeō* (pronounced or-thot-om-eh'-o) meaning "to cut straight, to proceed on straight paths, hold a straight course, doing right, to make straight and smooth, to handle aright, to teach the truth directly and correctly."[4]

Perhaps you can see we've come full circle with the idea of cutting straight. How can you truly do that? Only with the help of others as Proverbs 27:17 told us—the right kind of others. Those who have your best interest in mind. Those who will help guide you, not only through the understanding of God's word, but also with the "how to" of applying God's word in your life. I would encourage you today to seek out the counsel you need—coaching that can help you reach your full potential to create the abundant life that Jesus promises each of us when we exercise our M.I.G.H.T. and pursue it.

Remember scripture tells us, **"Two are better than one; because they have a good reward for their labour."** (Ecclesiastes 4:9) No man is an island, and no one lives nor dies to themselves (paraphrased from Romans 14:7). We need each other. We all need a little help now and then, and isn't it better to be proactive rather than reactive?

When someone is reactive it means they are pursuing help after something has already gone wrong, so most of the help they get is in the clean-up stage. Because of the difficulty and resulting mistakes or failures, they have a mess to clean up, so a good portion of any help they receive must be focused on cleaning up or straightening out the mess first and then improving the situation. However, for those who can learn to become proactive, it means seeking help before something goes wrong. Hence, more of the energy and help they receive is applied to preventing the mistakes or failures before they occur, so the path is made straight before walking down it.

A prudent man foreseeth the evil, and hideth himself: but the simple pass on, and are punished. (Proverbs 22:3 and Proverbs 27:12)

Yes, you read that right, the verse is found in two places in the book of Proverbs and is identical in both places. God obviously feels this is a very important point to repeat it exactly. Let's be *prudent*, which means "careful, cautious, wise, and sensible,"[5] and let's be sure we are asking for and getting the help we need along life's journey. Proactively seek out an abundance coach who can assist you with becoming everything you were meant by God to become!

TAKE AWAYS

- We need each other in this journey of life to help us become the best version of ourselves that we can be.

- Those who are on a higher level than we are can assist us in the climb to reach the level they are on.

- The purpose of a coach is to help us work on our areas of weakness, maximize our strengths, and see the big picture as we pursue our goals. The purpose of a spiritual coach then is to help us connect every area of our lives to our spiritual core to fulfill God's purposes and allow his abundance to flow through us to others.

- By having coaches for every area of our lives, we improve our chances for abundance in those areas, but only to the extent they do not conflict or cause confusion. Therefore, having the proper spiritual core and connection and even the right spiritual coach is so important.

NEXT STEPS

Consider the areas in your life where abundance may be lacking. Could you use a coach to help you minimize your weaknesses and maximize your strengths? Have you ever thought about assembling a team of coaches for every area of your life? Sometimes these coaches come from people we already know, admire, and trust—through family members, friendships, bosses, and mentors. However, sometimes we need others with more professional expertise who are on another level and can help us with our climb. It might take the use of some of your resources to get that kind of help, but usually the rewards you receive are worth more than the price you pay.

Would you trust your financial abundance to your emotional counselor? Knowing most spending is done based on emotion, maybe you would if you had a spending issue, but most likely you wouldn't. Therefore, be sure to evaluate where you are getting advice from in your life. If you're not sure you are getting the best counsel currently, then think about where you can get better counsel. I would strongly recommend taking your concerns to the best counselor there is (he *is* called wonderful—Isaiah 9:6)—God. Talk to God in prayer about your needs and ask him for guidance in whom to contact for help. When in doubt, seek out others in that profession who also have a strong faith. When my wife and I needed some short-term marriage counseling to work out an issue, it was important for us to find a faith-based counselor so they would provide godly counsel rather than worldly counsel.

Lastly, if you don't think you need a coach, I simply ask you rethink that idea and take it to God in prayer. Even the highest producing athletes, CFOs, and business leaders surround themselves with experts who can help them improve even by a margin of 1 percent because they know over time those improvements will add to their overall abilities. God desires for you to experience abundance. He's helped define what that means, and he's opened the door of opportunity to help you obtain it, but he can't make you walk through it. Only you can do that.

TRANSITION

I hope since you've stuck with me this far, you'll stay with me to the end. We've learned such great things up to this point. Not only have we defined what abundance means from God's viewpoint, we've also discussed how to obtain that abundance, and how to maintain it. With so much ground covered, it can be a little overwhelming to retain and now implement it. Well, I've got a little secret for you in the next chapter about the best way to ensure you have learned the information and that it can have the fullest impact in your life. Join me in the next chapter to find out what it is.

16
SHARING WITH OTHERS

"When one teaches, two learn."
–Robert Heinlein

ONE THING I LEARNED from reading Stephen R. Covey's book *The 7 Habits of Highly Effective People* that has stuck with me throughout the years is that to learn, we should teach. When we convert from simply learning something to teaching it, we move or shift to another level or perspective of understanding the information. It forces us to see it in a different way and it helps us solidify our thinking about it. (By the way I highly recommend reading Stephen Covey's book, as it is filled with very practical advice to help with every area of life.)

I once had a pastor who said he believed we didn't really know what we believed until we voiced that belief. I think he was trying to say we have all these thoughts bouncing around in us about beliefs we may hold, but until we chose or are forced to express those beliefs to someone else, we never shore them up into something that is solidly presentable. We continue to allow them to bounce around and develop. However, the moment we express those beliefs to someone else, we start to set the thoughts in concrete. They may be changed at some later date after we have more or new information to consider. By putting a voice to our beliefs, we have something that can be brought back to us by others as a "you said" comment.

As we learn something new and think deeply about it, we begin developing beliefs around those thoughts. If we want those thoughts to become more solid and our beliefs to become more solid as well, then we should begin to teach them to others. This first allows us the opportunity to put our voice to those thoughts, thereby shoring up our beliefs within ourselves. Secondly, through the process of teaching and not just sharing it allows us to face questions from those we teach.

DO YOU HAVE A QUESTION?

Most will avoid teaching and default to sharing only, and there is a difference—in fact, there is a big difference. By sharing only, you avoid questions from others. You make statements and walk away. You don't dig deeper—you don't wait for a response to see if your statements had any impact on the one to whom the statements were made. However, effective teaching allows for exchange between the parties and this exchange typically takes place through the questions that are asked of the teacher.

A good teacher is not afraid of questions. Most of us are afraid of questions because we fear we don't know the answers. Unfortunately, our society suggests we must always have the answers to the questions. We are educated in school from kindergarten through college via the process of quizzes, exams, tests, and papers to provide answers as though we know it all. The truth is we don't! And we don't have to! Sometimes the best answer to a question is, "I don't know the answer to that question, but I will look into it," and then follow through by researching an answer to provide later.

On the other hand, some questions we receive are only meant to tear down and disrupt or prove the speakers point. These types of questions may not even deserve an answer. Again, our society has drilled into us that we should answer every question asked of us. Really? Is it necessary to answer every question asked of us? Was this Jesus's practice when he walked the earth? On the day of his judgment before his crucifixion scripture tells us, **"When Pilate heard of Galilee, he asked whether the man were a Galilaean. And as soon as he knew that he belonged unto Herod's jurisdiction, he sent him to Herod, who himself also was at Jerusalem at that time. And when Herod saw Jesus, he was exceeding glad: for he was desirous to see him of a long season, because he had heard many things of him; and he hoped to have seen some miracle done by him. Then he questioned with him in many words; but** *he answered him nothing.***"** (Luke 23:6–9) (Emphasis mine.)

Even in the most desperate of situations Jesus found himself in, not every question asked of him required an answer. We must discern when a question is authentic and deserving of an answer and when it is not. Usually this can be determined by the phrasing of the question and the obvious intent of the questioner (by way of tone, expression, choice of words, etc.). If the question comes from a true desire to know more and learn, then the likelihood is the question is authentic and should be answered.

ONLY YOU CAN REACH THEM

Other than solidifying our own beliefs when we teach others, why should we teach the things we are learning? The second most important reason is because it might be the only opportunity those we teach have to receive the information in a way that only you can present it. You might be the one to get through to them. God has allowed them to be a part of your circle of influence in order that you might reach them. It's been his design from the very beginning—what we call word-of-mouth advertising. One tells another, who tells another, who tells another. If he hadn't designed it this way, he would have spoken to the world all at once himself. He is the only one with the power to do so, but he didn't—he's counting on you to be his mouthpiece. All you have to do is open your mouth and share.

I also believe through teaching we can advance levels. If we don't have actual experience in something, since experience helps move us forward to another level, then teaching can help replace experience because of the solidifying effect it has on our thoughts and beliefs—just like experience has on them.

When we hear the word "teaching," we should not be caught up in the formality of it. We may think, *I can't teach because I'm not formally trained to be a teacher.* If formal training is important to you, then get some, but also understand it is not necessary. God has given us all the ability to teach, simply by sharing our experiences in our own words. We can even teach others by our example when we are fully aware of doing so and that is our intent as we perform our actions.

NOT SURE WHAT TO SAY?

Still, scripture tells us that we can trust God to help us with the words we need when we teach others, even when we're not sure what to say.

> Now therefore go, and I will be with thy mouth, and teach thee what thou shalt say. (Exodus 4:12)

> I will instruct thee and teach thee in the way which thou shalt go: I will guide thee with mine eye. (Psalm 32:8)

Blessed be the Lord my strength which teacheth my hands to war, and my fingers to fight. (Psalm 144:1)

For the Holy Ghost shall teach you in the same hour what ye ought to say. (Luke 12:12)

Once when my kids were very young (ages four and two), we traveled from Wisconsin to New Jersey to visit some friends who had relocated there a few years earlier. We wanted to introduce our youngest child to our friends. To make the trip more affordable I arranged to preach at a church in the area. I am someone who likes to be prepared, so I prayed for weeks before the trip about what I should preach. However, I didn't receive any direction from God.

When it came time for the church service, and I still hadn't heard from God regarding my sermon topic or scripture passage I was very nervous, but I trusted God would deliver. My friend drove me to the service, and we arrived about thirty minutes before it was scheduled to start. After some small talk with the pastor, I dove into some final alone time with God in prayer. As those minutes ticked away, I got more and more nervous and felt so unprepared.

Finally in the five minutes before the service was to start, I felt God direct me to preach on a certain story from the Old Testament. I breathed a sigh of relief because I knew God had given me direction, even though I wasn't sure what exactly I was going to say. I knew he would prompt me as I went along. And he did. It ended up being one of the best messages I preached in my life, or should I say it was one of God's best messages because I truly felt that he was speaking through me. Therefore, believe me when I say you should step out and try it even when you're not 100 percent confident.

We should also keep in mind we have an ultimate responsibility to teach our children according to scripture.

And thou shalt teach them diligently unto thy children, and shalt talk of them when thou sittest in thine house, and when thou walkest by the way, and when thou liest down, and when thou risest up. (Deuteronomy 6:7)

Another reason we should step out and teach others the things we are learning is that we must teach to offset the incorrect teachings of others. It may be the only way we get the right information out there for others to know.

That they teach you not to do after all their abominations, which they have done unto their gods; so should ye sin against the Lord your God. (Deuteronomy 20:18)

Then will I teach transgressors thy ways; and sinners shall be converted unto thee. (Psalm 51:13)

And they shall teach my people the difference between the holy and profane, and cause them to discern between the unclean and the clean. (Ezekiel 44:23)

But in vain they do worship me, teaching for doctrines the commandments of men. (Matthew 15:9)

Whosoever therefore shall break one of these least commandments, and shall teach men so, he shall be called the least in the kingdom of heaven: but whosoever shall

do and teach them, the same shall be called great in the kingdom of heaven. (Matthew 5:19)

Lastly, it was also a direct commandment by Jesus for us to go and teach.

Go ye therefore, and *teach all nations*, baptizing them in the name of the Father, and of the Son, and of the Holy Ghost: *Teaching them* to observe all things what-soever I have commanded you: and, lo, I am with you alway, even unto the end of the world. Amen. (Matthew 28:19–20) (Emphasis mine.)

You're probably wondering why so much about teaching in a book about abundance. It's because I really want this informa-tion to get into you and sink down deep into your spiritual core, transforming from simple student to teacher will expedite the information. I'm not expecting you to become a group teacher or lecturer on the subject, but rather that you will pick out a thing here or there that spoke to you or resonated within and share the idea with someone else in your daily conversation or begin modeling it before those around you.

Teaching also embodies the very heart of abundance. Remember the definition of abundance? In its very basic terms, it's having more than enough to meet needs and then using the extra to help others. Applying this idea of abundance to information and learning, the information we receive allows us to learn and grow. Retaining that information for ourselves only would be the equivalent of hoarding, and we know that's not a good thing. Hence, the next logical thing to do is release the information back into someone else so they too can learn and benefit as we have. Therefore, abundance is self-generating or multiplying in this way.

TAKE AWAYS

- When we commit to sharing what we are learning with others—teaching—we give ourselves an opportunity to solidify our beliefs. We end up putting our beliefs into words, where they become concrete and help shape who we truly are.

- We shouldn't be afraid of questions when we realize not every question is deserving of a response. We should only feel obligated to answer genuine questions, those that are motivated by a desire to learn and gain new information to improve.

- We have been given opportunities by God to reach the people closest to us. God designed it this way. If we don't share with them, they may never know. Therefore, we should willingly teach through word and example those within our circle of influence.

- Teaching does not have to be difficult nor formal. It can simply be communicating our own experiences and things we have gained insight on with others through everyday language. However, the best way of teaching others is by our living example.

- When it comes to the things we're learning about God and sharing him with others, we don't even need to worry about what we are to say. God will provide the words at the moment we open our mouths to speak. How awesome is that!

- We teach because it embodies the heart of abundance. When we have learned and especially when we have implemented what we've learned, we have a reserve of knowledge that if we keep to ourselves, is a form of hoarding. Sharing our knowledge should simply spill out of us because we have more than enough—we have an abundance.

NEXT STEPS

Take a moment and think about things you have been eager to share with others. Usually behind the excitement to share is the desire that they would be able to experience what you have experienced. This is the purpose of teaching. Now that you have gained some knowledge about abundance through your reading of the previous pages, what are a few nuggets you can share with those closest to you? Decide on one thing you have learned and choose one person with whom you can discuss it. After the conversation, think about any deeper insights or reinforcements you received, then allow this to spur you on to share more with others.

TRANSITION

I am so proud of you that you have accompanied me through all this information. I appreciate your willingness and commitment to learn and grow. I trust as you implement this information, that you will see your life overflowing with abundance. I believe you will speed up that process when you share this learning with others. As we wrap up our journey together, I'd like to leave you with a few encouraging thoughts in the next chapter.

17
SOME WORDS OF ENCOURAGEMENT

"Everyone has inside them a piece of good news. The good news is you don't know how great you can be! How much you can love! What you can accomplish! And what your potential is."

—ANNE FRANK

I WANT TO THANK you for taking this journey with me and allowing me to speak into your life regarding abundance. I truly believe God's desire is for his people to live in an abundant way. It doesn't glorify God when people are only getting by in life or are suffering lack. On the other hand, it does glorify God when his people trust and obey his word, knowing that God will not only supply their needs but help them excel.

Please don't misunderstand me. I am not promoting some sort of prosperity doctrine. I believe I've already addressed that in previous chapters. What I am saying is that God acts toward us as the loving Father that he is. Many people think of God as some eternal judge looking down from the portals of heaven waiting for his creation to mess up so he can smite them. If this is our view of God, then how do we view ourselves as parents? Most of us see ourselves as loving, caring parents who only desire the best for our children. We want to see them succeed and be better than we are. Therefore, since God is our loving Father and he wants the best for us, we can trust he wants us to live in abundance. Otherwise, he would not have made the statement in John 10:10, which we have studied throughout this book. Let's look at that statement one last time.

The thief cometh not, but for to steal, and to kill, and to destroy: I am come that they might have life, and that they might have it more abundantly.

We obviously see God warns us about the intent of the thief, which is to harm us and take away our abundance. But we also see Jesus arrived on the scene to correct the situation and provide us life—but not the basic, ordinary, just-getting-by kind of life. Rather, God wants us to experience life to the fullest, to enjoy abundance so we can bless others with it and help them experience God for themselves. The Bible is full of other encouraging scriptures to help motivate us to realize who we are when we are connected to Christ.

But God, who is rich in mercy, for his great love wherewith he loved us, even when we were dead in sins, hath *quickened* us together with Christ, (by grace ye are saved;) and hath raised us up together, and made us sit together in *heavenly places in Christ Jesus.* (Ephesians 2:4–6) (Emphasis mine.)

The phrase "hath quickened us together" in the Greek is *syzōo-poieō* (pronounced sood-zo-op-oy-eh'-o) and means "to make one alive together."[1] Hence, we get the idea that this abundant life cannot occur without our connection to Christ. We come alive together with Christ.

Yes, Jesus came to give us life and we can comprehend and appreciate that through the sacrifice he made for our sin.

As a result, we can experience a better life in the present, as well as in the hereafter. However, we cannot experience abundant life without a complete intertwining of ourselves with Christ.

We must be willing to surrender our mental and emotional, relational and social, spiritual, physical, and financial selves to God's perfect will to see these areas flourish and experience the abundance God can deliver. It's not easy, as we've pointed out, and it takes work to surrender daily—in fact, every moment of every day. Every day or even several times throughout our day we are faced with a decision or decisions that must be made to allow God's will to be done over ours. This is the reason the apostle Paul made the statement, **"I die daily"** (1 Corinthians 15:31b), because he knew how important it was that God's will prevail in his life to accomplish all God wanted to do through him.

The choice is yours. You can decide how much of God you want by determining how close to God you will draw through prayer and Bible study. But you can also determine how much of God's will can be performed through your life by your willingness to become obedient to his word and what he speaks into your life. He usually gives us clues about what he wants to accomplish in us through the abundance he allows us to experience.

> **Then said Jesus unto his disciples, "If any man will come after me, let him deny himself, and take up his cross, and follow me."** (Matthew 16:24)

Notice this charge was given by Jesus not to those who needed to believe in him and the importance of his message, but it was given to his *disciples*. The disciples were those who already believed in him and were willing to follow him and be impacted by his words. They were those who wanted to be close to him. Jesus recognized their desire for closeness, but he urged them on to abundance and abundant living by denying themselves—the first step in obedience to God.

The phrase "let him deny" in Greek is *aparneomai* (pronounced ap-ar-neh'-om-ahee) meaning "to forget oneself, to lose sight of oneself and one's own interest."[2] By doing so, they could take up their cross, meaning face their challenges, realizing that it wasn't an easy thing, and then they would be able to truly follow him. The word "follow" in Greek here is *akoloutheō* (pronounced ak-ol-oo-theh'-o) and carries with it the idea of "not just following but reaching, to join as an attendant, to accompany, and a union, as to be in the same way with."[3]

Thinking in simple terms, when you follow someone, you are a step behind in a reactionary mode. If they step left, only after that do you step left. But Jesus wants us to be in union with him, to know his will for our lives before it's actually executed. In other words, Jesus is saying if we want to be in lockstep with him and thereby step left just as he is stepping left rather than afterward, we need to surrender completely and allow him to move in and through us. This is how he raises us up to those heavenly places, mentioned in Ephesians 2:4–6. The will of God comes directly from heaven and can only be executed in and through us, not by God lowering himself (he already did that through his atoning sacrificial death) but by lifting us up to where he is. He'll only do that for those who have denied themselves and taken up their cross to surrender completely to him. This demonstrates to

God our deep love for him and when we do that, scripture promises abundance will flow.

But as it is written, Eye hath not seen, nor ear heard, neither have entered into the heart of man, the things which God hath prepared for them that love him. (1 Corinthians 2:9)

God is preparing you for abundance, but it takes exercise on your part to receive it and utilize it wisely for the good of others. You may even be a little afraid not knowing what to expect or how to use God's abundance in the correct way. But realize that for those who have completely sold out to God, this does not need to worry you, because he will also direct your steps and help you in every area, even in your abundance.

A man's heart deviseth his way: but the Lord directeth his steps. (Proverbs 16:9)

ABUNDANCE RESPONSIBILITY

With abundance comes a certain responsibility from God's point of view. We understand this when we read the parable about the ten talents found in Matthew 25:14–30:

For the kingdom of heaven is as a man travelling into a far country, who called his own servants, and delivered unto them his goods. And unto one he gave five talents, to another two, and to another one; to every man according to his several ability; and straightway took his journey. Then he that had received the five talents went and traded with the same, and made them other five talents. And likewise he that had received two, he

also gained other two. But he that had received one went and digged in the earth, and hid his lord's money. After a long time the lord of those servants cometh, and reckoneth with them. And so he that had received five talents came and brought other five talents, saying, Lord, thou deliveredst unto me five talents: behold, I have gained beside them five talents more. His lord said unto him, Well done, thou good and faithful servant: thou hast been faithful over a few things, I will make thee ruler over many things: enter thou into the joy of thy lord. He also that had received two talents came and said, Lord, thou deliveredst unto me two talents: behold, I have gained two other talents beside them. His lord said unto him, Well done, good and faithful servant; thou hast been faithful over a few things, I will make thee ruler over many things: enter thou into the joy of thy lord. Then he which had received the one talent came and said, Lord, I knew thee that thou art an hard man, reaping where thou hast not sown, and gathering where thou hast not strawed: and I was afraid, and went and hid thy talent in the earth: lo, there thou hast that is thine. His lord answered and said unto him, Thou wicked and slothful servant, thou knewest that I reap where I sowed not, and gather where I have not strawed: Thou oughtest therefore to have put my money to the exchangers, and then at my coming I should have received mine own with usury. Take therefore the talent from him, and give it unto him which hath ten talents. For unto every one that hath shall be given, and he shall have abundance: but from him that hath not shall be taken away even that which he hath. And cast ye the unprofitable servant into outer darkness: there shall be weeping and gnashing of teeth.

We see in this story that the "Lord" (God) gave away talents to his servants. In other words, they experienced abundance for they had something that did not belong to them, above and beyond what they needed for themselves. What then was the expectation from their Lord? That they would share that abundance so there would be a return on the original abundance. I know many will look at this story in simply financial terms about the investment and say the return is the interest or the profit made. Others will look at it as the talents (abilities) God gives them and how they are to use them for God's glory. Both conclusions are correct; however, I'm asking you to dig deeper and think in terms of what I have been saying throughout this book. In every area of our lives when God allows us to experience abundance, it's not just for our benefit but rather it's for the benefit of others that they too may experience God and his goodness. In the story of the talents, it further illustrates we have a responsibility to ensure we are using our abundance for God's glory. Others are added to his kingdom when we do.

BE AN ABUNDANCE SPONGE

I want to share another thought with you. I jotted down this thought before I started typing the first chapter of this book. I had no idea where it might be useful, but now it is the very last thing I'm including. So here it is—you must be like a sponge when it comes to abundance.

A sponge was designed and created to soak up enough to be useful in a messy situation. Life can be messy. We've all experienced that. When you experience God's abundance, he has designed it for you to share it to help with the messy lives of others. But a sponge must be periodically renewed or rinsed out. Proper maintenance of the sponge keeps it useful. It's a cycle—soak—help—rinse—repeat. The cycle of abundance is to enjoy the blessings of God, share them with others, seek God's will, and stay close to be refreshed. Troubles and difficulties will come to help us value God's blessings and allow this to occur again and again in our lives.

Abundance can only last within the cycle. A broken cycle will disrupt the abundance. Soaking up abundance only for yourself leads to apathy and a lack of satisfaction because there's no usefulness. Helping others with total disregard of your own needs results in a messy life since it only transfers troubles from one to another. Rinsing only, that is only seeking God's will and relationship with never applying any action or assistance to others, results in a lack of joy. Only the full cycle allows for the full celebration of abundance for all, first for you in true fulfillment of being able to give, and then for others because of the blessings they receive.

I trust this book has helped you see the reason for God's abundance in your life in a slightly different light, and I also trust that God can and will give you the strength to carry that abundance for the benefit of others.

I can do all things through Christ which strengtheneth me. (Philippians 4:13)

I also believe you have seen the importance of asking for help when needed, as well as the significance of sharing what you have learned with others. I just want to leave you with one last encouragement from scripture.

And thou shalt love the Lord thy God with all thine heart, and with all thy soul, and with all thy *might*. (Deuteronomy 6:5) (Emphasis mine.)

I find it interesting that this admonition is found in Deuteronomy 6:5. The word Deuteronomy means "second law" and the book entitled Deuteronomy is the fifth book of the Torah or the Old Testament law that was given to Moses for the Israelites by God. It was this law that instructed them how to be obedient to God. So, we could say the first law was obedience for the sake of getting to know God. It was this law that enabled them to stay out of trouble and see God's favor and grace. But this law did not enable an in-depth meaningful relationship with God.

It was only through the "second law" which was a law coming from the place of love rather than strict obedience that made the way for real relationship with God. You see, genuine love moves someone to *want* to be obedient rather than *having* to be to stay out of trouble. And it's in that place of love that the two genuinely in love become one with each other. They can finish each other sentences, they can move in the same direction without resistance, and they can create possibilities beyond themselves—which is abundance.

When we fall in love with God and surrender everything that we are to him, we will experience the depths of his grace, because he loves and accepts us as we are. The only requirement for experiencing this tremendous grace, love, and abundance of God is for us to exercise our M.I.G.H.T.!

God Bless!

Pastor Rick

END NOTES

CHAPTER 1

1   Oxford Lexico, s.v. "life (n.)," accessed January 7, 2022, https://www.lexico.com/en/definition/life.

2   "H7965–Šālôm–Strong's Hebrew Lexicon (NIV)." Blue Letter Bible, accessed January 7, 2022, https://www.blueletterbible. org/lexicon/h7965/niv/wlc/0-1/.

3   "G2072–Esoptron–Strong's Greek Lexicon (KJV)." Blue Letter Bible, accessed January 7, 2022, https://www.blueletterbible. org/lexicon/g2072/kjv/tr/0-1/.

CHAPTER 2

1   Oxford Lexico, s.v. "promise (n.)," accessed January 7, 2022, https://www.lexico.com/en/definition/promise.

2   "G2222–Zōē–Strong's Greek Lexicon (KJV)." Blue Letter Bible, accessed January 7, 2022, https://www.blueletterbible.org/ lexicon/g2222/kjv/tr/0-1/.

3   "G4053–Perissos–Strong's Greek Lexicon (KJV)." Blue Letter Bible, accessed January 7, 2022, https://www.blueletterbible. org/lexicon/g4053/kjv/tr/0-1/.

4   "H5397–Nᵊšāmâ–Strong's Hebrew Lexicon (NIV)." Blue Letter Bible, accessed January 7, 2022, https://www.blueletterbible. org/lexicon/h5397/kjv/wlc/0-1/.

5 Oxford Lexico, s.v. "abundance (n.)," accessed January 7, 2022, https://www.lexico.com/en/definition/abundance.

6 Oxford Lexico, s.v. "happy (adj.)," accessed January 7, 2022, https://www.lexico.com/en/definition/happy.

7 "G1097–Ginōskō–Strong's Greek Lexicon (KJV)." Blue Letter Bible, accessed January 7, 2022, https://www.blueletterbible.org/lexicon/g1097/kjv/tr/0-1/.

CHAPTER 3

1 Oxford Lexico, s.v. "exercise (n.)," accessed January 7, 2022, https://www.lexico.com/en/definition/exercise.

CHAPTER 4

1 Furey, Robert. The Joy of Kindness. Crossroad, 1993,193.

2 Oxford Lexico, s.v. "resolve (v.)," accessed January 7, 2022, https://www.lexico.com/en/definition/resolve.

CHAPTER 5

1 "G509–Anōthen–Strong's Greek Lexicon (KJV)." Blue Letter Bible, accessed January 7, 2022, https://www.blueletterbible.org/lexicon/g509/kjv/tr/0-1/.

2 "H5397–Nᵉšāmâ–Strong's Hebrew Lexicon (NIV)." Blue Letter Bible, accessed January 7, 2022, https://www.blueletterbible.org/lexicon/h5397/kjv/wlc/0-1/.

3 "G4151–Pneuma–Strong's Greek Lexicon (KJV)." Blue Letter Bible, accessed January 7, 2022, https://www.blueletterbible.org/lexicon/g4151/kjv/tr/0-1/.

CHAPTER 7

1 "G4995–Sōphronismos–Strong's Greek Lexicon (KJV)."
Blue Letter Bible, accessed January 7, 2022, https://www.
blueletterbible.org/lexicon/g4995/kjv/tr/0-1/.

2 "H7941–Šēḵār–Strong's Hebrew Lexicon (NIV)."
Blue Letter Bible, accessed January 7, 2022, https://
www.blueletterbible.org/lexicon/h7941/kjv/wlc/0-1/.

3 "G3631–Oinos–Strong's Greek Lexicon (KJV)." Blue Letter
Bible, accessed January 7, 2022, https://www.blueletterbible.
org/lexicon/g3631/kjv/tr/0-1/.

CHAPTER 8

1 "Discernment Definition & Meaning." Merriam-Webster,
Merriam-Webster, https://www.merriam-webster.com/
dictionary/discernment.

2 "G3056–Logos–Strong's Greek Lexicon (KJV)." Blue Letter
Bible, accessed January 7, 2022, https://www.blueletterbible.
org/lexicon/g3056/kjv/tr/0-1/.

CHAPTER 9

1 "G5384–Philos–Strong's Greek Lexicon (KJV)." Blue Letter
Bible, accessed January 7, 2022, https://www.blueletterbible.
org/lexicon/g5384/kjv/tr/0-1/.

2 "G4382–Prosōpolēmpsia–Strong's Greek Lexicon (KJV)."
Blue Letter Bible, accessed January 7, 2022, https://www.
blueletterbible.org/lexicon/g4382/kjv/tr/0-1/.

3 "Favorite Definition & Meaning." Merriam-Webster,
Merriam-Webster, https://www.merriam-webster.com/
dictionary/favorite.

4 "G1448–Engizō–Strong's Greek Lexicon (KJV)." Blue
   Letter Bible, accessed January 7, 2022, https://www.
   blueletterbible.org/lexicon/g1448/kjv/tr/0-1/.

CHAPTER 11

1 "H5869–'Ayin–Strong's Hebrew Lexicon (NIV)."
   Blue Letter Bible, accessed January 7, 2022,
   https://www.blueletterbible.org/lexicon/h5869/kjv/
   wlc/0-1/.

2 "H3893–Lēaḥ–Strong's Hebrew Lexicon (NIV)."
   Blue Letter Bible, accessed January 7, 2022,
   https://www.blueletterbible.org/lexicon/h3893/kjv/
   wlc/0-1/.

3 "H5127–Nûs–Strong's Hebrew Lexicon (NIV)."
   Blue Letter Bible, accessed January 7, 2022,
   https://www.blueletterbible.org/lexicon/h5127/kjv/
   wlc/0-1/.

4 Josephus, Flavius, and William Sanford La_Sor.
   "Antiquities of the Jews, Chapter 5." The Complete
   Works of Josephus, Kregel, Grand Rapids
   (Michigan), 1995, pg. 70.

CHAPTER 12

1 "Abundance Definition & Meaning." Dictionary.
   com, Dictionary.com, https://www.dictionary.com/
   browse/abundance.

2 "G3623–Oikonomos–Strong's Greek Lexicon (KJV)." Blue
   Letter Bible, accessed January 7, 2022, https://www.
   blueletterbible.org/lexicon/g3623/kjv/tr/0-1/.

CHAPTER 14

1 "G3525–Nēphō–Strong's Greek Lexicon (KJV)." Blue Letter Bible, accessed January 7, 2022, https://www.blueletterbible.org/lexicon/g3525/kjv/tr/0-1/.

2 "G1127–Grēgoreō–Strong's Greek Lexicon (KJV)." Blue Letter Bible, accessed January 7, 2022, https://www.blueletterbible.org/lexicon/g1127/kjv/tr/0-1/.

CHAPTER 15

1 "H1270–Barzel–Strong's Hebrew Lexicon (NIV)." Blue Letter Bible, accessed January 7, 2022, https://www.blueletterbible.org/lexicon/h1270/kjv/wlc/0-1/.

2 "H6440–Pānîm–Strong's Hebrew Lexicon (NIV)." Blue Letter Bible, accessed January 7, 2022, https://www.blueletterbible.org/lexicon/h6440/kjv/wlc/0-1/.

3 "Discernment." The Free Dictionary, Farlex, https://www.thefreedictionary.com/discernment.

4 "G3718–Orthotomeō–Strong's Greek Lexicon (KJV)." Blue Letter Bible, accessed January 7, 2022, https://www.blueletterbible.org/lexicon/g3718/kjv/tr/0-1/.

5 "Prudent." The Free Dictionary, Farlex, https://www.thefreedictionary.com/prudent.

CHAPTER 17

1 "G4806–Syzōopoieō–Strong's Greek Lexicon (KJV)." Blue Letter Bible, accessed January 7, 2022, https://www.blueletterbible.org/lexicon/g4806/kjv/tr/0-1/.

2 "G533–Aparneomai–Strong's Greek Lexicon (KJV)." Blue Letter Bible, accessed January 7, 2022, https://www.blueletterbible.org/lexicon/g533/kjv/tr/0-1/.

3 "G190–Akoloutheō–Strong's Greek Lexicon (KJV)." Blue Letter Bible, accessed January 7, 2022, https://www.blueletterbible.org/lexicon/g190/kjv/tr/0-1/.

ACKNOWLEDGMENTS

My HEART OVERFLOWS WITH an abundance of gratitude for all those who have helped me on both my life's journey and the process of writing this book.

Thank you to all my relatives, teachers, pastors, friends, and co-workers who have taught me lessons and given me opportunities to practice along the way.

Thank you to Brett Hilker and the Self-Publishing School team for coaching me through the process of writing this book.

Thank you, Tina Pocernich from Wandering Words Media, for your editing expertise and helping to make this work a readable book.

Thank you, Jodi Giddings, for your wonderful layout skills in making the presentation of this book fabulous for the reader to enjoy!

Thank you to my amazing launch team. Just having you in my corner, knowing you were willing to help me get this book out into the world, kept me inspired and moving forward.

Lastly, thank you reader for taking the time to read this book and for considering how this information can impact your life. I pray you find an abundance of God's Spirit influencing you and directing you to greater levels of sharing with others.

EXPERIENCE GOD'S PROMISES FOR YOURSELF!

Communicating with God should be easy right? Then why do we find it so difficult, especially when it comes to knowing why or how to pray?

We all want the promises of God to be fulfilled in our lives, but did you know the key to releasing them is found through prayer?

IN GOD'S PROMISES: A PRAYER JOURNAL, YOU'LL FIND:

- A short study on prayer so you can understand the importance of prayer.
- Prayer templates to help you find words to communicate with God yourself.
- A methodology to discover how God responds to your prayers.
- Space to journal and express yourself to God.

Learning the importance of prayer and how to actually pray can release the power of God in your life in amazing ways. If you utilize this prayer journal, you will begin to see just how God is meeting you in your times of devotion and that He truly responds to your prayers.

Anytime, anywhere, God is waiting to hear from you. Start communicating with Him today and learn how He responds to you. Read Pastor Rick's *God's Promises: A Prayer Journal* to grow your prayer habit and feel God's power.

Order your copy today at www.WisdomWell.guru/products

ABOUT THE AUTHOR

PASTOR RICK STEPHENSON has two grown children and lives with his beautiful wife in Johnson Creek, Wisconsin.

As a licensed minister with the Assemblies of God, Pastor Rick refers to himself as a worship evangelist, combining his musical ability with his motivational speaking talents. He travels the US to preach the gospel and enjoys seeing people be impacted by the power of God. He has witnessed numerous individuals healed and restored through his services, for which he gives all the glory to God. As a worship leader, he writes original spirit-filled contemporary Christian worship music. Pastor Rick has released four full-length albums as well as two EPs, won several songwriting awards, and received airplay in both the US and overseas.

In addition to being a minister, Pastor Rick is a certified master financial coach, experienced CPA, CMA, and real estate agent. He is also the CEO of Wisdom Well Abundance Coaching, LLC, and is passionate about helping people experience the most out of life. He teaches his clients how a spiritual center can help balance all areas of life, resulting in improved relationships, mental clarity, and greater physical health.

If you're interested in learning more about how Pastor Rick can help you in this way, visit **www.WisdomWell.guru** today!

YOUR TURN TO SHARE
THE ABUNDANCE!

THANK YOU FOR READING MY BOOK!

I truly appreciate all your feedback and I love hearing what you have to say.

I need your input to make the next version of this book and my future books better.

Please take two minutes now to leave a helpful review letting me know what you thought of the book:
(**https://www.wisdomwell.guru/review**)
Thank you so much!

Pastor Rick Stephenson

WHAT'S NEXT
SIGN UP FOR ABUNDANCE COACHING!

WISDOM WELL

I love working with those who are interested in pursuing the abundance of God. I provide coaching to help you on your journey from both a spiritual and practical perspective. From my background of over thirty years in finance and business and over twenty years as a licensed minister, I can provide sound advice to help you navigate the difficulties of life.

SET UP A CONSULTATION TODAY:

https://calendly.com/rick-stephenson

Website: www.WisdomWell.guru

I look forward to talking with you!

Pastor Rick Stephenson

www.ingramcontent.com/pod-product-compliance
Lightning Source LLC
Chambersburg PA
CBHW071145130626
46553CB00004B/1533